OASIS

OASIS

Lee Henshaw

This edition published 1996 by
Parragon Book Service Ltd
Unit 13-17 Avonbridge Trading Estate,
Atlantic Rd, Avonmouth
Bristol BS11 9QD

Produced by Carlton Books
20 St. Anne's Court
London W1V 3AW

ISBN 0.75251.859.3

Printed and bound in Italy

Acknowledgments
The publishers would like to thank the following sources for their kind permission to reproduce
the pictures in this book:

All Action/Chris Floyd, Tony Kelly, Justin Thomas; London Features/Kristin Callahan, David
Fisher, Joe Hughes, Colin Mason, Ilpo Musto, Mike Prior, Derek Ridgers, Tom Sheehan; Pictorial
Press/Rob Verhorst; Retna/Bill Davila, Steve Double, Pat Pope, Paul Slattery, Chris Taylor; Rex
Features/ Dave Hogan, Nils Jorgensen, Hayley Madden, Brian Rasic, Richard Young, Jon Shard;
S.I.N/Piers Allardyce, Marina Chavez, Melanie Cox, Martyn Goodacre, Antony Medley, Ian Tilton,
Kim Tonelli.

Special thanks are due to Paul Slattery (represented by Retna Pictures) for allowing us access
to his Oasis tour photographs.

Every effort has been made to acknowledge correctly and contact the source and/or copyright
holder of each picture, and Carlton Books Limited apologises for any unintentional errors or
omissions which will be corrrected in future editions of this book.

contents

better than the wendys

The first article I ever wrote for the national press featured Oasis. It was September 1994 and the band were three singles old and being hailed as The Next Big Thing. My piece for *The Observer* wasn't actually about Oasis, it was to do with another Manchester institution: In The City, the annual British music industry convention founded by then head of decaying Factory Records, Anthony Wilson.

Pete Tong, Radio 1 jock and chief talent spotter at London Records, remembered that Oasis had played at the event two years earlier as an unsigned band that 'couldn't get arrested'. Oasis were one of twelve unsigned bands to play the inaugural In The City in 1992, and those few members of the music industry that did see them passed on them.

Just four years later Oasis are massive, the only band of the moment likely to repeat the amazing success of the Beatles three decades earlier; evidence that the music industry is notorious for getting it wrong and that these stars of pop were anything but an overnight success.

It was over six months after the In The City gig of May 18 1993 when Alan McGee, seeing Oasis play at Glasgow venue King Tut's Wah Wah Hut, declared: 'I've found the greatest rock'n'roll band since the Beatles.' McGee was head of Creation Records — an indie at the time, and home to Primal Scream, the Boo Radleys and Jesus & Mary Chain, among others. It was later

Noel sports his mono-brow

'I've found the greatest rock'n'roll band since the Beatles': Alan McGee, Creation Records (pictured right).

paul bardsley on noel in 1985

the same year that the label would jump into bed with the Sony corporation.

McGee had picked up on a band with the temerity to look and sound as if they knew they'd be the first great British pop group of the Nineties. Not that it should have surprised him — the Oasis brothers, Noel and Liam Gallagher, had been at it for years. Before they met McGee, their story was very much a Manchester one.

The original members of Oasis — the band have since lost one member and recruited a southerner — all spent their formative years living in the Manchester suburb of Burnage. Noel recalls first plucking on the guitar at the age of eight. Liam would have been three.

'Someone showed me "The House Of The Rising Sun" and I never looked back,' he says. At thirteen he wrote his first song. Called 'Badges', it was about people who wore them.

Paul Bardsley, vocalist with Manchester's now defunct Molly Half Head, and presently between bands, remembers jamming with Noel Gallagher: 'I think it was 1985 or 1986, when Mike Tyson came onto the scene. There was a lot of kids who played football together in Burnage and me and Noel were in that gang, we'd play guitar and sing a little bit. We had a stupid name, it was Fantasy Chicken and The Amateurs.'

Noel and his little brother have progressed some since then. Oasis are the band of the moment. Champions of the post-rave generation, they've conquered the British singles chart, released the fastest-selling debut album of all time, transformed a once-credible Blur into their poor relatives, dominated the acclaim of the public and the pundits for their second album, *(What's The Story) Morning Glory?*, and entered the record books again by playing to 80,000 people over two nights at Manchester City's football ground, Maine Road.

Away from home Oasis have one more stumbling block to confront — achieving stadium status in America — before comparisons with the Beatles are truly founded.

Before Oasis played that fateful gig at King Tut's Wah Wah Hut, like the Smiths, the Happy Mondays, and the Stone Roses before them, they'd struggled to get the movers and shakers of Manchester's music industry on their side, with Noel employing what lessons he'd learnt about the music industry from Manchester stars Inspiral Carpets. He wanted to be their singer, but ended up as chief roadie between December 1988 and December 1992. 'Do you know when the Lockerbie plane

The first Oasis line-up: Noel Gallagher, Paul McGuigan (Guigsy), Paul Arthurs (Bonehead), Liam Gallagher and Tony McCarroll.

crash was?' asks Inspiral's Clint Boon, unsure of the exact date he struck up a relationship with Noel. 'That was the night when we auditioned him to be the singer,' he says about Noel's attempt to fill a vacancy eventually occupied by Tom Hingley.

'We didn't want him [Noel] to sing with us because he wasn't the kind of singer we were after, even though he could sing, after a fashion, as they say,' remembers Clint. 'We all liked him, though, so we said, "If you want to work for us we're going to need a roadie."'

Before this audition Noel had been working for the Gas Board as a watchman at their Manchester City Centre depot on Little Peter Street. Liam, then sixteen, took over his job when the Inspirals made Noel their runner and roadie.

'He was the first proper employee we had,' says Clint. 'He was never just one of a team of roadies, he was always much more than that. He had a full-time job and a full-time wage.' (Sources say he was on the very tidy sum of about £500 a week.) 'He took in everything he saw us doing. We included him in a lot of business stuff, he knew

Noel's early employers, the Inspiral Carpets.

I **learnt** that you'll get **ripped off** unless you're very **careful.** And I **learnt** that **all** record **company** people are *****, bar none.

noel gallagher

how much we were getting off publishing and record companies, we told him all that stuff, and he took it all in and stored it away for the future.'

'I learnt that you don't make money unless you're as big as U2,' says Noel. 'I learnt that you'll get ripped off unless you're very careful. And I learnt that all record company people are twats, bar none.'

Put on earth to dig holes
Beyond developing some acumen for the business of music, while he was with the Inspiral Carpets, Noel also struck up a relationship with monitor engineer Mark Coyle, who was to co-produce the first four Oasis singles. Once they'd set

It's a family affair. Liam and Noel with brother Paul and mum Peggy after a home town gig.

The Gallagher home in Burnage.

up the Inspirals' gear, Noel and Mark would play Noel's tunes. 'I heard them talking about Bacharach and the Beatles a lot of the time,' says Clint Boon, 'and sometimes after the sound check they'd be sat in the dressing room playing acoustic guitar, singing Beatles' songs. Noel used to tinker on the gear and write his own songs. I couldn't give you any titles, but he did have recognizable tunes that he'd play every night that were part of his catalogue.'

At the close of 1991 Noel returned from a European tour with the Inspirals to discover that Liam was singing with his band, Oasis. His fellow members — Paul McGuigan (Guigsy) on bass, Paul Arthurs (Bonehead) on guitar and Tony McCarroll on drums — had previously been members of Manchester band Rain; not to be confused with a band of the same name from Liverpool.

11

Dumb. One of the dozen or so bands that shared rehearsal space with Oasis in the early days

Oasis played their first gig (with and without Noel) at Manchester venue the Boardwalk.

Tony French, who had played the program drum machine for Rain before they got in Tony McCarroll recalls: 'Rain was originally Tony McCarroll, Bonehead, Guigsy, and Chris Hutton was the singer. Then Liam came down to see them recording in the basement of Raffles hotel. He had a word with Paul and Bonehead, and the band disbanded and started again with Liam as singer. I think Liam had told them he'd try and get Noel in on it as well.'

Paul Gallagher, Liam and Noel's older brother, remembers how much Liam wanted Oasis to succeed. 'When he finished work he'd come home and say, "I wasn't put on this earth to dig holes", which was typical of him. Liam was always a cocky little so and so, but I always knew he would make the band happen.'

It was at the Boardwalk on August 18, 1991, that Oasis played their one gig without Noel. They were supporting Sweet Jesus. Noel was in the audience with members of the Inspiral Carpets, and brother Paul. 'Rain was fucking crap,' remembers the eldest, and equally candid Gallagher brother. 'When Liam joined the name was changed to Oasis straight away. It was taken from the Swindon Oasis, which was a venue in Swindon,' he reckons, probably aprocryphally.

Noel recalls how the band got their name rather differently. 'It's from a shop in town where we buy our trainers. The name doesn't actually mean anything, but it means something to us. Oasis was the only shop in town that used to sell really good trainers imported from Germany. Even when I was younger and into punk they used to sell Sex Pistols T-shirts.'

Clint Boon's feelings about the Oasis gig were similar to Paul Gallagher's: 'Noel had asked us to go along,' he recalls, 'and I don't think anyone was particularly impressed, but then after that Noel started talking about kicking them into shape by reshaping things.'

The luckiest man

Oasis, with Noel, began rehearsing at the Boardwalk, adjacent to other Manchester bands, Dub Sex, the Houndgods, the New Fads (Fast Automatic Daffodils), Detox and Sister Lovers. Although it's been reported that one of these bands left the message 'get your own riffs' on the door of the Oasis room, this message was actually posted to the New Fads by Detox; the two bands feuded to the extent of bricking up the entrances to each other's rehearsal rooms.

Paul Gallagher remembers Oasis rehearsing up to six nights a week at this time. 'They were just rehearsing, rehearsing and getting it right,' he says. The band were to record their first demo before Christmas 1991 at the Abraham Moss studios. It was picked up and played by Signal Radio jock Craig Cash and Pete Mitchell of Key 103. 'It wasn't actually very good,' Pete recalls, 'but I do remember Craig wanting to get Liam for the band he managed, That Uncertain Feeling.'

Embarrassed by the content of that tape, Noel would later deny in an interview with Pete Mitchell that he actually played on that tape, despite the fact his brother Paul confirms he did.

In the Christmas 1991 edition of the Manchester listings magazine *City Life*, Chris Sharratt, then music reviewer, described 'Colour My Life', the first track on that recording, as 'a bit nasally in places, sort of like Dermo from Northside but with a cold, and in fact the whole song is in that Northside vein. The second track's ['Take Me'] a bit more urgent and weird, sort of Inspirals on psychedelics. Interesting, but I'm not too excited'.

When Oasis played their first gig with Noel at The Boardwalk in January 1992, their first song was 'an instrumental without lyrics', says Paul Gallagher of 'Columbia'. Noel took the songwriting credit. A shrewd decision on his part — it's the writer who reaps the

> You **pick** up your **guitar**, rip a few **people's** tunes **off**, **swap** them **round** a bit, **get** your brother in the **band**, **punch** his **head** in every **now** and **again**, and it sells.
>
> **noel gallagher**

publishing money rewards. Martin Fisher also worked for the Inspirals at the same time as Noel. 'Even back then,' he recalls, 'Noel was saying the only reason he was doing Oasis was to get in there to make as much money as possible... and leave some really good tunes behind.'

Paul Gallagher prefers to remember Noel as the obvious choice for the role of songwriter. 'I've got a very early tape of Noel recording his own song on a four-track around 1989. I knew he could write songs, I knew he could sing songs. His voice wasn't very strong, so knowing Noel as I do he would have thought, "I'll write the songs, the band will be my engine, Liam can be the face and the voice.'"

Quizzed about this decision Noel replies, 'Why? Because I'm stubborn. I don't like anybody else's music apart from the Beatles, and I couldn't be in a band if I couldn't write the music and the words... not the words so much, but our kid had a go at that and they were pretty poor so I thought, "well I better do that and all."

'All I ever wanted to do was make a record,' he says. 'Here's what you do: you pick up your guitar, you rip a few people's tunes off, you swap them round a bit, get your brother in the band, punch his head in every now and again, and it sells. I'm a lucky bastard. I'm probably the single most lucky man in the world — apart from our Liam.'

Factory interest

The first record company to believe the music and the attitude had merit was Manchester label Factory Records. In the Summer of 1992, Phil Saxe, talent scout for the label, wanted to put Oasis on a Factory sampler. It was something that would never happen, because the label was poised for bankruptcy. 'The first time I remember hearing the name Oasis was when I got a phone call at home from Clint Boon of the Inspirals,' he says. 'Clint said to me: "Phil, I'm in Amazon studios at the moment with this band, Oasis, they're not getting anywhere, no one's interested, can you help them out? They're a really good band." Now at that time I knew Ian Brody was in the other studio at Amazon, and he'd been told by MCA he could have his own label, so I said to Brody: "Can you go and see if there's anything decent about this lot?" But nothing came of that so I took it on my mind to have a look at them.

'I went to see them supporting Real People at the Boardwalk, and I really loved them,' continues Phil. 'The first thing Liam said to me was "fuckin' hell we're better than The Wendys", which was a bit nasty seeing as I managed The Wendys at the time. I loved them, you know, I tend to understand them very well. I liked the way they used to wear Marks & Spencer's checked shirts. At the time me and Tony [Wilson] were talking about doing a

Liam and Noel had told me they were going to tell that lot at Factory where to get off because they wouldn't sign to them anyway.

paul gallagher

compilation album, getting loads of bands on one album, and one of the bands I wanted to do was Oasis.

'I got told after Adventure Babies that we couldn't sign anyone else because we had no bleedin' money,' he says. 'Our financial position was perilous, I knew that because I hadn't been fucking paid for about four or five months. I'm not saying anything would have come out of it, because we probably would have had Oasis too soon, but yes we were there, we had a little part to play.'

Axe man and songwriter Noel Gallagher.

Tony Wilson's Manchester label, Factory Records, were the first to express an interest in Oasis, then they went bust.

Keyboard players don't look cool onstage, they just keep their heads down. There has never been a cool keyboard player, apart from Elton John.

noel gallagher

Anthony Wilson recalls that Factory were the first label to express interest in Oasis but 'not enough fuckin' interest'. 'There were two bands that Phil Saxe wanted to sign at the time,' he says. 'Oasis and Pulp. It was Phil's job to give me cassettes, and the Oasis one was the one I liked, but I was too busy with the lawyers going bankrupt.'

'Privately Liam and Noel had told me they were going to tell that lot at Factory to fuck right off because they wouldn't sign to them anyway, because anyone who gives eight-hundred grand to the Happy Mondays deserves to go bust,' offers Paul Gallagher — his insight into relations between Factory and Oasis.

In the city

Noel spent the remainder of the summer smooching with those members of Manchester's music industry who shared his enthusiasm for the band. One of them was Penny Anderson, a music journo who occasionally filled in for Terry Christian on his weekly music column for *The Manchester Evening News*, *The Word*. Penny interviewed the band for *The Word* in June 1992, their second ever interview with the press — they had previously featured in the now defunct Manchester lifestyle magazine, *Uptown*. In the article — titled, 'Just when the

Blessed Ethel win best band award at In The City 1993. The music industry ignore Oasis once more.

music scene was drying up...The refreshing sounds of Oasis' — Noel revealed why the Oasis sound was one fuelled by the traditional line-up of vocals, guitars, drums and bass. 'I've always been into guitars,' he said, 'we want to put keyboards on, but keyboard players don't look cool onstage, they just keep their heads down. There has never been a cool keyboard player, apart from Elton John.'

Speaking to Penny a year later Noel would discuss why the acoustic bent, one that has since contributed to shaping perceptions of the Oasis sound, was so important to him. 'I respect songwriters,' he said. 'I can't stand Bob Dylan, but I like his songs, most other indie bands hide behind distorted guitars, and loads of shouting.'

Two other people attracted to Oasis were Macca — then manager of Factory Records' Manchester pretenders,

Once upon a time Oasis played to hundreds, not thousands.

Northside — and his partner in the management company Caromac, Caroline Elleray.

'Macca knew Noel really well,' says Caroline. 'Noel gave him a tape, I think "Rock'n'Roll Star" was on there, and we went down to see them rehearse at the Boardwalk. I was sharing an office with Mark Riley at the time, who was just getting *Hit The North* [the Radio 5 show] together with Mark Radcliffe, and I said to Mark, "get them in on session", and he did.' The session was broadcast during July 1992. 'I think they played "Cigarettes And Alcohol",' she recalls, 'and the best thing is, the BBC have lost the tape. The first ever broadcast Oasis radio session, it would be worth a mint!'

Caromac didn't manage Oasis. Caroline didn't have the money to develop them, and Macca was worried about Northside because they were signed to Factory Records, which was in decline. In the autumn Noel was to approach Bindi Binning about a gig. Bindi was one of the coordinators of the unsigned-band nights for In The City, 1992. 'I only put on four bands, and they were one of

them,' says Bindi. 'Skywalker, Machine Gun Feedback, Jealous and Oasis at The Venue on September 13, 1992. Although their demo wasn't great, they were one of the best of the local acts around,' she says. 'I remember Noel gave it me and I had a final slot to fill, and chose them. The gig wasn't brilliant, Liam's vocals were really off, and I don't think they went down really well at all.'

'I'd brought a load of A&R down,' says Caroline Elleray who was still championing the band's cause. 'WEA, Rondor, Silvertone, London, loads of them. Like Noel said, it was the night that they got turned down by the music industry, who'd all said they sounded too much like the Stone Roses. I remember Liam was moving about around the stage quite a lot, his stage technique is pretty cool now compared to then.'

Ever to their defence, Paul doesn't remember the band being bothered by this rejection. 'They wasn't arsed,' he recalls.

No smiles from Oasis.

On the carpet

Oasis existed but Noel Gallagher did not earn a salary from the band, and for the last two months of 1992 he was back on roadie duty, touring Europe with the Inspiral Carpets. It was to be his final job with them. At the end of the tour the Inspirals announced they could no longer accommodate their road crew's drug habits and laid them all off, including Noel. This was no sudden fit of conscience. According to Mark Hoyle of Manchester band Dumb, whose previous band, Dub Sex, had been supported by the Inspirals in 1987, 'they were very anti-drugs all the time... Inspirals always were'.

'It wasn't something we could accommodate any more really,' says Clint Boon. 'I mean we all loved him, he was part of the brotherhood and stuff, but we couldn't

19

handle it any more. It was a very amicable split, and it's probably the best thing that ever happened to him.

'It was hard, he was a friend, someone we had always got along with,' continues Boon, 'and it was on the eve of us going to America. He did have something else to focus on, though, and we gave him a golden handshake, a really, really big golden handshake. We felt bad about it but we didn't lose a lot of sleep over it.'

Noel freely admits to some heinous drug offenses in his time with the band. 'Here's a secret,' he recalls about border crossings with the Inspirals. 'The band never knew this, right, but we used to stash the drugs on them. We're going across borders and some official would come on and check the bus, then afterwards one of the band would say, "Where did you hide the drugs?" We'd just put our hands underneath his pillow and say, "Just there!" I think that's why we got the sack in the end.'

It was also at the close of 1992 that Oasis, particularly Noel, built a relationship with Real People, a Liverpool band. Tony Griffiths, their singer, has reason to believe that Oasis were the beneficiaries of Real People's production aspirations. 'When the Real People were on tour with the Inspiral Carpets we'd meet Noel,' says Tony. 'We went to see Oasis after they'd got sacked by the Inspirals [Liam was also, though more casually, an Inspiral roadie] at the Boardwalk in Manchester. That's the first time I saw them playing live, and they were fairly dreadful. They only had two songs, "Rock'n'Roll Star" and 'Bring It On Down', the rest of it was very mediocre.

'We'd just set up a studio in a warehouse on the Dock Road in Liverpool — it was only an eight-track — and we basically spent a full three months producing Oasis. Liam had never sung with headphones on before so Chris, me brother, had to basically sing the songs and say to Liam, "Sing it like that." People have always said that Liam sounds like our Chris... maybe that could be one of the reasons why.

'I remember,' he continues, 'it was quite funny at the time, because Liam kept freaking out. He kept on taking the headphones off and saying "Fuckin' hell man, I can't do

Liam had never sung with headphones on before so Chris, me brother, had to sing the songs and say to Liam, "Sing it like that." People always said that Liam sounds like our Chris... maybe that could be one of the reasons why.

tony griffiths (real people)

The tambourine man.

that." I think he was off his head at the time, so that didn't help. It was three months of starting at seven at night and finishing about seven in the morning.'

In with a chance

The result of these sessions with the Real People was the demo *Live Demonstration*. Finished by early 1993, most songs on it appeared later either as B-sides or as tracks on *Definitely Maybe*. 'Cloudburst' was a B-side on 'Live Forever', 'D'Yer Wanna Be A Spaceman' on 'Shakermaker', 'Columbia' was the band's first white label, and 'Bring It On Down', 'Married With Children' and 'Rock'n'Roll' star made it to the first album. 'Fade Away' was an additional track on the CD-single 'Cigarettes And Alcohol'.

Little was happening for Oasis outside of Manchester and Liverpool at the beginning of 1993 until they played a gig on May 18 at King Tut's Wah Wah Hut in Glasgow. Manchester band Sister Lovers were booked, and took Oasis along with them, where they also played with Boyfriend and new Creation Records' signing, 18 Wheeler.

The deal was all in support of 18 Wheeler, but it was to be a better deal for Oasis, although it very nearly didn't happen, as Al Smith, Sister Lovers' drummer, recalls. 'We were sharing a rehearsal room with [Oasis] at the Boardwalk, and we had this gig at King Tut's supporting 18 Wheeler, and they wanted another band for it so we asked Oasis. They said yes. We get to the gig and the promoter had already got another band, and he said Oasis couldn't go on.'

Despite reports to the contrary, Oasis were unaware that Alan McGee, the Creation Records supremo, was going to be at the gig. Tony French, who designed the cover for *Live Demonstration*, the twisted Union Jack that would become the Oasis logo, was part of a fifteen-strong posse that went up to Glasgow with the band. 'We got there and Noel said, "We're on tonight" and the manager said, "Sorry mate, no you're not,"' he recalls. 'Noel said, "I've sorted it out with one of my friends, that's not on." Noel had a little word in his ear saying, "Look, there's fifteen of us here. If you wanna kick us out it's going to kick-off!" Basically the manager said, "I'll give you a fifteen-minute slot — you'll have to go on

We told the promoter that if Oasis didn't play then we wouldn't, and because we were mates with Boyfriend they said they wouldn't play if we didn't.

debbie turner, on the gig that made oasis

Liam Gallagher proves static is cool.

first." So they went on, and there was only about six people in there, and that guy, Alan McGee, must have come in and caught the last couple of tunes. I remember Noel giving him a copy of *Live Demonstration* after the gig.'

Debbie Turner, who was vocalist with Sister Lovers (she presently fronts Manchester band Slot Machine), claims that McGee turned up at the gig 'with his sister to see one of his bands, 18 Wheeler'.

'I don't think he knew we were on and he definitely didn't know Oasis were playing,' she says. 'There was supposed to be four bands playing — us, 18 Wheeler, Boyfriend and Oasis — but when we got there the promoter told us, "There's no way that other Manchester band are playing as well." The reason they did play is because we told the promoter that if Oasis didn't play then we wouldn't, and because we were mates with Boyfriend they said they wouldn't play if we didn't. It didn't actually happen the way it's usually told.'

The most exciting band

Noel's memories of the gig are similar: 'We weren't even supposed to be playing on the bill. We were told we were, then when we got there, we were told we weren't, so we threatened to... well, you know. So they only let us on for twenty minutes. We did four songs, one was 'I Am The Walrus' by the Beatles. It was the worst gig we've ever done. Then we just came off the stage, and got a deal.'

'Oasis are the most exciting new band I've seen since 1989,' said McGee after the gig. 'There's no limit to their potential. I knew within one song that they were a great band.'

Liam, the singer with the thick Northern drawl, was the component of Oasis that most impressed McGee. 'I'd just arrived and I'd heard about this band, and how they were going to trash the gig, and I thought this sounds great, like the Sex Pistols or something,' says McGee. 'When I arrived, I saw fifteen lads around a table, and one of them looked amazing. He had this blue-and-white Adidas top on and he looked really cool, like Paul Weller or something. He turned out to be the singer.'

A friend of McGee's, Nathan McGough, once manager of the Happy Mondays, and presently part of East West

When the boys arrive at Creation they're less than impressed with the company MD, **Tim Abbott.** He's **wearing** a **Manchester United top...** they are **cocksure** enough to tell **McGee** they'll only **sign** if Abbott **takes** that **shirt off."**

paul gallagher

Records' A&R squad, was used to Alan McGee's enthusiasm over new bands. 'Alan is always euphoric about every band he signs. He rang me after that gig and said, "Have you heard of Oasis?" I said, "Yes." He said, "Well I've just signed them and they're going to be the next Beatles." And I said, "You say that about every single band you sign." And he said, "Yeah, but this time I really mean it."'

McGee may have been thrilled with his new find, but the band were less impressed. Paul Gallagher's commentary on their reaction to McGee's advances and offer of a trip to

London to visit Creation records hints at overtones that are not dissimilar to those of the Beatles towards manager Brian Epstein's first approaches to them, decades before. 'McGee said to them, "Do you want a record deal?" and they said, "Who the fuck are you?" He said "I'm Alan McGee from Creation," which didn't really inspire them. Anyway, they got back and said, "We've been offered a record deal by some cunt called Alan McGee." The next day McGee rang Noel and said there were four train tickets waiting for him at [Manchester] Piccadilly station. Noel didn't believe him until he actually got on the train and arrived at Creation with Liam and Bonehead.

'When the boys arrive at Creation they're less than impressed with the company MD, Tim Abbott,' Paul continues. 'He's wearing a Manchester United top. Oasis are massive City fans, and despite Creation being the only label expressing any interest in them at that time they are cocksure enough to tell McGee they'll only sign to his label if Abbott "takes that fuckin' shirt off".'

In search of management

By June relations between Creation and Oasis were being cemented by members of the band and the label indulging in all-night drinking sessions. So confident that his band was destined to be the biggest in the world, Noel insisted that if Oasis did sign to Creation it would be written into the contract that he would receive a chocolate-brown Rolls-Royce once they became 'massive'.

It was also in June that Oasis met Marcus Russell, the man who was to become their manager. Despite interest from Creation, Oasis were still without management and, among others, Noel approached In The City's Bindi Binning about the role. 'I know they'd asked loads of people in Manchester to manage them, and everyone rejected them,' recalls Bindi. 'Then they approached me and Anthony Bogiano [a band manager who had looked after the Inspiral

Johnny Marr introduced Noel to his future manager, Marcus Russell.

25

Live my life in the city, there's no easy way out: 'Rock'n'Roll Star'.

Future's looking so bright...

Carpets for a while]. They gave us the tape, *Live Demonstration*, and I adored it, and I was really into doing it. I thought Liam was a star even then. I really wanted to manage them, but that was the week Noel met his all-time hero, Johnny Marr, and he thought it would be cool to have Johnny Marr's manager handle them.'

Johnny Marr was drawn to Oasis in the coincidental manner that Alan McGee happened upon the band. Noel had met an old friend at the Manchester club, the Hacienda, someone he had known only as 'Ian'. Noel told him about *Live Demonstration* and this Ian asked him for a copy to give to 'our kid', who turned out to be his younger brother, Johnny Marr. Marr had once been guitarist with the Smiths and then one half of Electronic, with Bernard Sumner of New Order. After listening to the tape, Marr rang Noel and the two discussed, among other subjects, the fun that could be had with vintage guitars. Marr also said he would mention Oasis to his manager, Marcus Russell.

Russell and Marr saw Oasis play at the Hop and Grape in Manchester, supporting Dodgy, in June of 1993. Although Oasis and Russell's company, Ignition Management, are still not tied contractually, he has represented Oasis since that night.

When word of McGee and Russell's interest reached the rest of the music business, a bidding war for Oasis began. U2's Mother Records allegedly offered the band double whatever Creation could muster. Such promises proved insufficient to entice them away from Creation, a label they believed shared their megalomaniac tendencies. Oasis wanted to conquer the world.

September 14, again as part of In The City, Oasis played as part of a 'Creation Night' at Manchester's Canal Cafe Bar, together with Medalark 11 and 18 Wheeler. On October 22, 1993, Oasis signed to Creation for Britain, with Sony getting rights to the rest of the world. The contract was for six albums.

I **told** Noel, you're **paying £300** a day here to **record** a **pile** of *****, why **don't** you do **something** really worthwhile? **And** that's **basically** where **"Supersonic" came** from.

tony griffiths (real people)

Powerhaus, Dave Massey, head of Sony America, declared, 'It was the best first gig I've seen. I started jumping around because every song was a hit. And they had the best eyebrows I'd ever seen in my life.'

Not B-side the point

In the hands of Creation, Oasis began a low-key tour. As Noel said in an interview given in June 1993 before the band had signed to Creation, Oasis had played most gigs in Liverpool to get a better audience than they could achieve in their home city. In Manchester often it was only a gaggle of friends who whould turn up to watch the band. 'The one thing I'll say about [Manchester] is that all the regular venues which put on local bands' nights charge £3.50 to get in, £2.50 for a beer,' he said. ' I wouldn't go and see local bands and spend six quid in the first half an hour, unless they were mates. You go to Liverpool and it's a pound to get in, a pound for a drink, and you get about 150 people in, as opposed to playing in Manchester to ten people who don't want to see you.'

On this first record company-funded tour, Oasis supported Liz Phair, the Milltown Brothers, the BMX Bandits, CNN, Saint Etienne and the Verve. On December 16, 1993 they supported Real People at the Krazy House in Liverpool. After this gig they went to record some tracks for Creation at the Pink Museum studios, with Real People as their producers again.

'Oasis had told us we could help them out with some B-sides,' recalls Real People's Tony Griffiths of a session that wasn't expected to yield any Oasis singles. 'They booked into the Pink Museum studios for three days with Creation paying for it,' he says, 'and they only had two songs, one which was an acoustic song and one which had a really dated Manchester indie sound, a really crap song it was.

'I couldn't really believe they were recording these songs. But they were saying "they're only B-sides", so I had to point out there's no such thing any more as *only*

Bass man Paul 'Guigsy' McGuigan.

had to point out there's no such thing any more as *only* B-sides. When you put on a CD you don't have to physically turn the thing over, the songs just come on, so "B-sides" are very important.

'I told them the songs they were doing were a load of crap and said to Noel: "What was that thing you were jamming before? The one that sounded a bit like Neil Young?" And he said, "That one's not finished." I said, "Look, you're paying £300 a day here to record a pile of shite you're not going to be happy with, why don't you do something really worthwhile, write a song, make a song out of it." And that's basically where "Supersonic" came from.'

Drunk and disorderly

While Oasis were recording in Liverpool, Creation began a marketing campaign the like of which had not been seen since the launch of the Smiths — and the Sex Pistols, the Beatles and the Rolling Stones before them. To chosen record companies Creation released 'Columbia', the track the band had recorded at the beginning of the year for *Live Demonstration*. Back when Noel had just joined the band, 'Columbia' was an instrumental but, as Tony Griffiths claims, during the recording of *Live Demonstration* Chris Griffiths wrote the lyrics for its first verse. Paul Gallagher contradicts this: '"Columbia" the song was written by Noel, "Columbia" the lyrics was written by Liam, but [Chris] wouldn't get out of the studio while they were recording it, so they gave him a credit on it.'

Whoever really wrote the song, BBC Radio 1 took an unprecedented step and play-listed this one-sided piece of vinyl, despite its not being available commercially. Gary Blackburn, Creation's plugger responsible for convincing radio stations of the band's potential, recalls, 'When we first heard the Oasis tapes over at Creation, Alan McGee said, "Right, Gary, you're at

Wembley. It's the World Cup final. The ball's on the penalty spot and there's no goalkeeper. If you stick this one away, you've won the cup." And it turned out to be like that.

'We started off with this white-label of "Columbia",' he continues, 'took it to a few radio stations, and they put it on the play list straight away.'

'Columbia' was early evidence of the band's influences. The track is reminiscent of George Harrison's 'It's All Too Much' from *Yellow Submarine*, a piece of LSD-inspired psychedelia written in 1967. Like the Beatles and the Stones, Oasis wanted enough recorded material to release a single every two months, and an album, in the following year — in 1994 they managed five singles and the album.

Finishing at the Pink Museum studios, Oasis went to Monrow Valley studio in Wales to record the songs they needed. They arrived on January 7, 1994; eighteen days later they had little music to offer Creation. There was a formative 'Slide Away', some Stones' covers, with Noel singing and the cover photograph for 'Supersonic', which was taken there.

Next Oasis moved to London's Olympic studios, where after only four days they decided they did not want to work with producer Dave Bachelor. Instead they recruited Mark Coyle, who had worked with Noel during his days with the Inspiral Carpets, and left London. Over ten days in February Oasis recorded most of the tracks for their debut album, *Definitely Maybe*, at the Sawmills Studios in Cornwall.

Apart from those recording sessions, the first two months of 1994 were quiet by the standards Oasis had begun to set. Eager to gig outside Britain, they decided to play Holland. An ambition that was tempered when the Dutch police arrested everyone except Noel before they had set foot off the boat.

Guitar heroes, Noel and Bonehead.

rock 'n' roll pigs

The eventual rise of Oasis in popularity is attributable to more than their music, there are also their lifestyle and attitudes to take into account. Oasis, to borrow a Liam Gallagher phrase, are 'mad for it'. To make their reinterpretation of musical precedents complete even before releasing their first commercially-available single, Oasis were pursuing the kind of extra-curricular activities that have always defined 'sex, drugs and rock'n'roll'. Their first reported kick-off happened on 18 February, 1994.

The band were scheduled to support the Verve in Amsterdam, their first gig outside Britain. When the ferry

taking them to Holland arrived, only Noel got off — the rest of the band had been forcibly detained.

It seems that while Noel was getting some sleep the others took advantage of duty free prices — as much as four litres of Jack Daniels and a couple of bottles of champagne have been suggested. Steamed up, they were alleged to have got in a fight with some Chelsea supporters. By morning, Liam, Bonehead, Guigsy and Tony McCarroll were in a dockyard cell waiting to be deported to Britain. The gig was cancelled.

In an interview with music paper *NME* a month later, in which Oasis were referred to as 'rock'n'roll pigs', Noel revealed he was a little less 'mad for it' than his brother. 'The thing about getting thrown off ferries and getting deported is not summat that I'm proud about,' he claimed.

Spot the 'Cigarettes And Alcohol'.

33

A fledgling rock'n'roll star: Liam at the Fleece And Firkin in Bristol during Oasis' March 1994 tour with Whiteout

Liam disagreed and a heated debate took place before the interviewer.

'He gets off the ferry after being fucking deported, and I'm left in Amsterdam with me dick out like a fucking spare prick at a fucking wedding,' shouted an angry Noel. 'This lot think it's rock'n'roll to get thrown off a ferry. And do you know what my manager said to him? He said, "Nah, rock'n'roll is playing in Amsterdam, coming back and telling everyone you blew them away, not getting thrown off the ferry like some scouse schleppers with handcuffs. I won't stand for it. It's football hooliganism."'

Four lads from Manchester getting into a fight on a boat wouldn't ordinarily be newsworthy. But this was Oasis, and even so early in their career some media people were interested in them, and Oasis promised to be a package worth getting excited about. They were only doing what they maintained they had always done; not just fighting and drinking, but drugs as well if they felt the need. They didn't intend stopping just because their band showed promise, and more importantly they didn't mind talking about it. Even to reporters. It was a hedonism that would threaten to split them apart on many occasions. Fortunately, Noel Gallagher always seemed to know when enough was enough. After all, he'd seen it all before.

'As a roadie with the Inspirals I've been to Argentina, Russia, Japan — all over the world. There is nothing that will shock me,' he says. 'I've done all the groupie shit that the rest of the band do and, believe me, I've had a great time. But I'm not in the band to sleep around. I am in it for

34

Rock'n'roll is about being yourself. I went on that boat, I had a drink. I had too much beer and I got in a fight, and that was it.

liam on visiting amsterdam

might as well do the white-line' — the first of many Oasis references to the drug that Sting described as 'God's way of telling you you've got too much money'.

At the end of March, however, Oasis made their TV debut on Channel 4's *The Word*. Liam Gallagher remembers the appearance as being pivotal. 'We come off *The Word* and, like, went on a little tour, and it was just mad. Loads of people turning up off that song, people who would never have heard you, only if they'd got on you when you were starting. Loads of people just turned up because they heard that song and they liked it. And it's top.'

Their appearance on *The Word*, their commitment to playing live, the support of the taste-defining *NME* and

two big reasons. I love music and I want to be very rich. I've been writing songs since my teens and I know that we can be big enough to let me retire on my own tropical island.'

Noel Gallagher's first attempt to secure Oasis a slot within contemporary culture (and make some cash) was 'Supersonic'. Before its April 11 release, the public had received only a few tasters of the Oasis sound, some radio sessions, the play-listed 'Columbia' and a tape attached to a February edition of *NME*, 'The Mutha Of Creation'. This intriguing item included a demo of 'Cigarettes And Alcohol', which contained the line 'you

**Is it my imagination or have I finally found something worth living for?
'Cigarettes And Alcohol'.**

Melody Maker — both papers gave 'Supersonic' Single Of The Week status — and a striking video took Oasis into the Top 40. 'Supersonic' peaked at No. 31.

The lyrics of 'Supersonic' owed no small debt to Shaun Ryder, fallen star of the Manchester movement, and John Lennon. Noel described the song as their 'I Am The Walrus'. It also promoted the feel-good factor, the cry of 'Feeling supersonic/give me gin and tonic' perfectly capturing their wanton spirit.

The supporting tracks were 'Take Me Away', an acoustic song with Noel taking the vocal role, their live slab of rock 'I Will Believe', and their previous white-label release, 'Columbia'. Every component of this record, from the posturing on the front cover to the swagger of the sound, suggested that Oasis were a band who had bought wholesale into the rock'n'roll experience. And so, it appeared, did those people looking for a taste of that decades-old tradition.

The wrecking crew

In March Oasis headlined across Britain, and the tour was a sell-out. 'It's gone mad,' said Liam Gallagher in a mid-tour radio interview. 'We've had, like, proper stage invasions the last two... fucking wild. You can't get off the stage because you've got to go through the crowd to get to where the room is. And you just can't get off the stage; everyone piling on the stage singing the songs, and that.'

The tour's first date had them at the Bedford Angel on March 23, 1994. Oasis played for £100, and after the gig, with fans in tow, retired to Bedford's most expensive hotel. The Moathouse's night porter didn't like them singing Beatles' songs in the corridors. The hotel — it was privileged to be the first — banned the band, but it was only a mild shenanigan; later there would be much rowdier incidents than this one. 'Me and Bonehead would just walk into a hotel room and empty it out the window,' says Noel

These could be the best days of our life: 'Digsy's Dinner'.

I've done the groupie bit... but I'm not in the band to sleep around. I am in it for two big reasons. I love music and I want to be very rich.

noel

about the Who-like relationship Oasis developed with hotel rooms at the start of their touring career. 'I would be doing interviews in my room or in the bar and halfway through one of the band would come in for a fag or something. I didn't suss out that they were seeing where I was sitting. So I'd be playing it all down, saying, "It's all been blown out of proportion. It's all about the music..." and the journalist would be thinking: "I'm sure I've just seen a TV set go flying past that window!"'

Noel Gallagher knows how to tell a good story. Not just with a song, but in interview. He is dry and he is witty, a trait of many who originate in the city where taking the piss is a preoccupation. He'll protest he prefers to talk about the music — 'You get into scrapes, but we're not in a band because of a certain lifestyle, we're in a band because of the music. If you want us to be the Happy Mondays then I'm afraid we're not going to be.'

But when he does talk about the exploits, he is forever fuelling perceptions of a lifestyle that mirrors the one the Rolling Stones led (who also had their moments with hotel rooms).

Starting with the debut tour, although many exploits were restricted to the music press, Oasis quickly became a focus for newsy column-inches at home and, increasingly, abroad. They walked the line (and snorted much of it) trodden by the Stones in the Sixties, Sex Pistols in the Seventies and the Happy Mondays in the Eighties. Oasis are the icons girls want to bed and boys want to be.

'Get a bit worried if boys started fancying me, definitely,' Liam replied to an interviewer suggesting that he might share the homophobic tendencies Shaun Ryder had expressed in his time. 'But they wouldn't be fancying *me*, though, would they? They'd be fancying *something*, but not me. They'd just be fancying that vibe, but they'd have to sort those fucking hormones out or something. I'm into the girls fancying me and stuff, mad for it.'

With all the new media interest, interviews were continually on the agenda. Liam, at least, had no ambitions to be an interview-wise repeat-Beatle when it came to talking to the press. 'I don't like talking about things like that,' he said, 'big issues and that, because I'm not into it. I've got nothing against gays, they do what they do, I do what I do... as long as they don't pinch me on the bum or whatever.'

In bed with Bonehead.

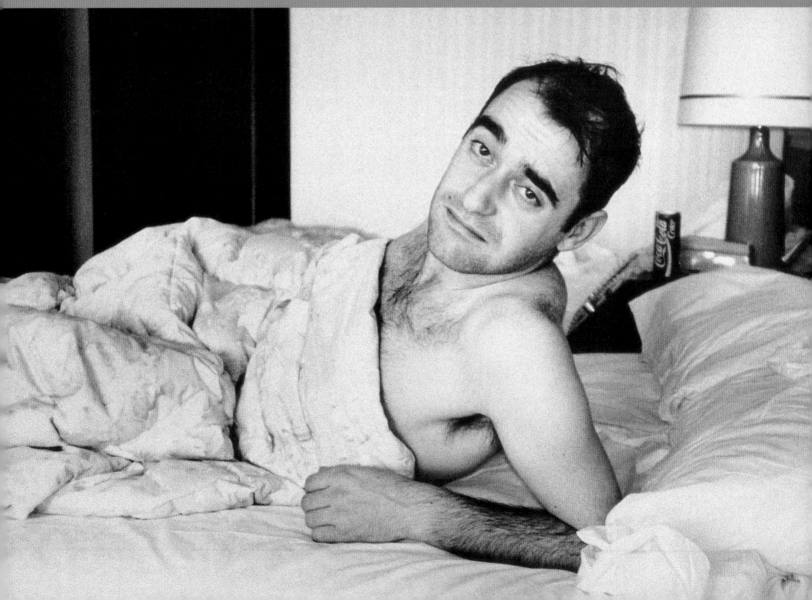

Beer bottles and stage invaders

Oasis weren't the only band exhibiting a rock'n'roll lifestyle. They had a session in August 1994 with the Verve after both bands had played the Hultsfred Festival in Sweden. (Oasis managed to get to, and play this first European date without incident.) Back at the hotel, the two bands were said to have taken alcohol from the bar, hurled bedroom fittings out of their hotel rooms and consumed no one knows what narcotics. They did attract the attention of the police. The Gallagher brothers — very lapsed Roman Catholics — were obliged to pay between £800 and £30,000 in compensation (depending which newspaper you read). It goes without saying that the hotel banned them. For a measure of that spectacle check out the cover to the fourth Oasis single, 'Cigarettes And Alcohol'.

The same month — in which their third single, 'Live Forever', went Top 10 — Oasis were also expelled and banned from the Columbia hotel in London. The band (minus Noel) threw beer bottles from their hotel room window at a Mercedes sitting in the car park below. It belonged to the hotel manager. While they were being ejected from the Columbia a bored Noel apparently wrote 'Some Might Say', a single the following year.

August 1994 also demonstrated that as well as creating a fracas, Oasis were capable of attracting trouble. During a gig in Nottingham a stage invader hit Noel in the face. Noel — appropriately in the middle of playing 'Bring It On Down' — didn't take it too well.

Tension had been building at the gig all night as some of the crowd tried to rile the band with chants of 'Man City, wank, wank, wank' and 'Soft as shite'. Noel remembers everything going smoothly until the middle of 'Bring It On Down'. 'I was doing the guitar solo and the guy just appeared. He was about two foot away from me, and I thought he was a stage diver. All of a sudden, I noticed he had this big ring on, he just smacked me in the eye... People were saying to us, "John Lennon would have gone on." No he wouldn't... I've only got two eyes, if one goes I don't get another one back, so at the end of the day it's only rock'n'roll and I'm not prepared to donate parts of my body for the cause.'

> I'm into the girls fancying me and stuff, mad for it. Get a bit worried if boys started fancying me, definitely. I've got nothing against gays... as long as they don't pinch me on the bum or whatever.

liam on his fans

He will fill it with drugs though.

'I suppose I should slow down,' concedes Noel, 'but I usually go mad for forty days and then I'm sensible for the next forty days. The chest pains and stuff don't bother me.

Medical science has come a long way. It's amazing what you can put yourself through and get away with. If my lifestyle ever affected my work I'd clean up, but it doesn't. We don't go onstage when we're out of it, we play totally straight.'

Walking the line

On record and on their records Oasis have acknowledged that cocaine is their preferred narcotic, and they don't appear to care who knows it: 'I put drug references in because I take them, and I write about what I know,' explains Noel.

About cannabis Noel says he's been smoking it since he was fourteen, non-stop, but he hopes 'they never legalize it, neither — it just mongs people out', and Liam concedes he took heroin when he was fifteen but now he 'wouldn't do it again because I'm better than that'.

'I don't mind this wild image that we've got because it's all true,' says Noel. 'The only person it bothers is me mam. She hits me round the head when she reads about me going to hospital and stuff, but I tell her, "I didn't collapse, I just fell down and couldn't get up for a while."'

'You looking at me?'

We don't deny the fact that we take drugs such as cocaine, marijuana and ecstasy,' he continues. 'We've been doing drugs since we were fourteen. In Manchester there are only three things you can do when you leave school — play soccer, work in a factory or sell drugs. You usually end up doing the third because you're no good at soccer, and you're not going to bother working in a factory. Drug-dealing is easier.'

Published comments like these were bound to attract unwelcome attention at some point, and following an interview in the *Melody Maker* in March 1996, Noel Gallagher received some he could have done without. Campaigner Dr Adrian Rogers, representing the Conservative Family Institute, took it upon himself to demand a police investigation into Oasis.

'What people have got to understand is that we're lads, We have burgled houses and nicked car stereos, and

Medical science has come a long way. It's amazing what you can put yourself through and get away with. If my lifestyle ever affected my work I'd clean up, but it doesn't.

we like girls and we swear,' said Noel. 'Most of the songs I write are under the influence of one thing or another.'

Dr Rogers made the connection that because of the band's massive popularity such admissions would prompt their fans to do exactly the same things. Not quite the

I'd like to teach the world to shop.

same hysteria that prompted Americans to burn Beatles' records after John Lennon's comment that they were bigger than Jesus, but nonetheless a knee-jerk reaction to a band who were now a part of popular consciousness.

'This is actually yobbish, criminal behaviour,' said Dr Rogers, 'and most young people don't want that, don't understand it and don't want to see a society that's based on it. But there are some rather simple-minded youngsters who will see this as a pinnacle of behaviour.'

This message was patronizingly mirrored by Ian Wardle of the drugs advice organization, Lifeline, 'They're relics from the Sixties,' he began. 'There is nothing new in Oasis rambling on about their predilection for drugs. It is like the Land That Time Forgot. This is the sort of thing that Keith Moon [the Who's legendary drummer] used to do.'

Creation issued a statement, their first to be scripted in defence of the band: 'The band have never made any bones about what they have done and what they do. Theirs isn't an unusual story for most kids in the country. The band and the songs are an example to people of what they can achieve. They put out a message that things are possible. Dr Rogers should check his facts, cos the British record industry is one of the country's great exports.'

In his own defence Noel Gallagher now says, 'I think you'll probably find that we're the most honest band around, I think everybody else is just lying. I know for a fact that you read interviews by these people who claim not to use drugs — they are liars. They are not only lying to their fans, they're lying to themselves. People go on about we brag about drugs. We don't. The thing is, people say to me, "Do you take drugs?" I say, "Yes I do." I think we just are what we are, people know where they stand with us.'

Between August 1994 and March 1996 actions, gestures and comments made by Oasis too numerous to mention would be catalogued by the media. But interest in these 'misdemeanours' would not have been sustained if the band hadn't followed up 'Supersonic' with some of this decade's most compelling songs so far.

Blurred distinctions

In the last half of 1994 Oasis had four singles — three made the Top 10 in Britain — and in *Definitely Maybe* the fastest-selling debut album of all time. Occupying a space in pop culture seemingly reserved for the Stone Roses, Oasis and the battling Gallagher brothers had arrived in some style. But there were more battles waiting for Mancunians who invaded southern turf.

The developing rivalry between Blur and Oasis was one that would eventually spark the biggest pop tiff of the Nineties — and since the legendary Beatles-Rolling Stones

'How does that one go again?' Noel and Bonehead at Creation's Undrugged night at the Albert Hall.

What people **have** got to **understand** is that we're **lads**, We have **burgled** houses and **nicked car** stereos, and **we** like **girls** and we **swear.**

`noel`

'I've got a mike stand, right, and that's what I'm into.'

battle for the charts in the Sixties. Its roots can be traced to back to the occasion of Creation Records' tenth anniversary celebrations. After the press conference announcing the forthcoming event to be held at London's Royal Albert Hall, Oasis retreated to the drinking place favoured by north London's pop leftfield, the Good Mixer in Camden Town.

Blur's Graham Coxon was also present, and Liam met him for the first time. He gave Graham a mouthful. (At this point Oasis had already decided that they hated Blur. Their tour-bus song — to the tune of the Small Faces' 'Lazy Sunday' — is 'Wouldn't it be nice, to be a fucking cockney/Wouldn't it be nice, to be in Blur/What a cunt'.) The crowd moved on to another joint, the Camden Underworld, where later Liam and the rest of Oasis were asked to leave after Graham complained about the constant verbal abuse he was getting from Liam.

On June 4, 1994 Bonehead and Noel played at Creation Records' anniversary concert at the Royal Albert Hall, Undrugged. They played their second single, 'Shakermaker', and aired the forthcoming singles, 'Live Forever' and 'Whatever'.

'Shakermaker', released June 20, 1994, owed a melodic debt to the New Seekers' 'I'd Like To Teach The World To Sing', which had become Coca-Cola's early-Seventies advertising jingle. Creation were worried the giant soft-drinks corporation might sue. They had reason — the band used the line 'I'd like to buy the world a Coke' when they played 'Shakermaker' live. However, no legal action ensued, and the single landed comfortably in the UK charts the next week at No. 20.

Oasis take T in the Park, summer 1994.

'Shakermaker" — arguably the poorest Oasis single to date — wasn't lacklustre enough to stall the hype machine that began to push the band towards dizzy heights. Its release prompted an appearance on BBC TV's *Top Of The Pops*, and later in the month their June 26 gig at the Glastonbury Festival was televized as part of Channel 4's *4 Goes to Glastonbury*.

At the festival Oasis played between Credit To The Nation and Echobelly on the *NME* stage. Noel almost missed taking part — only five minutes before the show he was discovered watching naked didgeridoo players in the Green Field. 'Are you gonna wake up, then, for some real songs?' Liam shouted at him.

The band were on a roll. Only three days earlier Noel had appeared live with Neil Young's backing band, Crazy Horses. A month later the band were in America, playing New York's New Music Seminar. 'My mam's dead proud of me,' Noel told *Melody Maker* that month. 'I've had my picture taken with Arthur Lee [of Love], I've been onstage with Crazy Horse and I'm going to have my picture taken with Johnny Cash. All I need now is my picture taken with Burt Bacharach and I've got the full set.'

In New York Oasis visited Strawberry Fields in Central Park, the memorial to John Lennon opposite the Dakota building where the Beatle was shot by an insane fan in December 1980. Appropriately it was also where they shot the video for 'Live Forever', their third single, released on August 8, 1994.

'Live Forever' gave Oasis their first Top 10 British hit... just, it made No. 10. Backed by an acoustic track, with Noel on vocals, 'Up In The Sky', a Stone Roses-like 'Cloudburst' and a live version of 'Supersonic', 'Live Forever' excited the music press enough for both *Melody Maker* and *NME* to run editions featuring Oasis on their front covers. The last band they had done this for was U2, in 1988. The anthemic 'Live Forever' proved that the band were at least as good, if not better, than their hype, and it proved to be the perfect prelude to the release of *Definitely Maybe* three weeks later.

Oasis' debut album cost them £75,000 to make, even though they had used a total of seven studios to record and produce it. The buzz surrounding its release on August 29, 1994 was massive. It sold over 150,000 copies in the first few days, making it the fastest-selling debut album of all time. *Definitely Maybe* entered the UK charts at No. 1, beating the popular operatics of the three tenors, Jose Carreras, Placido Domingo and Luciano Pavarotti, an unlikely set of rivals that prompted Creation to comment: 'Three fat blokes shouting are no competition for Oasis.'

On the release day the band played a live set for over a thousand fans at Virgin Megastore's Marble Arch branch in London. Playing acoustically, they went through 'Supersonic', 'Shakermaker', 'Live Forever', 'Sad Song', 'Slide Away', and when they played their future Christmas song, 'Whatever', they were joined onstage by Evan Dando of the Lemonheads.

Co-produced by Noel Gallagher and his mate from the Inspiral's days, Mark Coyle, with additional production and mastering by Electronic's producer, Owen Morris, *Definitely Maybe* didn't offer many new tracks for the die-hard fan.

Noel and Liam at Strawberry Fields, the John Lennon memorial park in New York.

'All I need **now** is my picture taken with **Burt Bacharach** and I've **got** the full set.'

There were only five that a keen collector wouldn't already have owned: 'Rock'n'Roll Star' (a track from their *Live Demonstration* demo), 'Cigarettes And Alcohol' (which would be the band's fourth single), 'Digsy's Dinner', 'Slide Away' and 'Married With Children' (also from *Live Demonstration*). Another previously unreleased number was 'Sad Song', which was only available on the vinyl release.

Despite the short supply of new material, the album was evidence that in the format they had chosen — the very traditional rock band line-up — Oasis excelled. *Definitely Maybe* was their *Revolver*.

Rolling stone roses

'Rock'n'Roll Star' is a song that affords hope to all the Oasis wannabees; empowerment is the message in its — and the album's — opening line: 'Tonight, I'm a rock'n'roll star'. But if 'Rock'n'Roll Star' is a classic, then so is 'Cigarettes And Alcohol'. The two are songs that define a moment, that capture the attentions of the post-rave, post-baggy generation and, like all the classic pop songs that had preceded them, they are difficult to forget. 'Cigarettes And Alcohol' was proof of the results that can be achieved with three chords and a record collection featuring the Beatles, the Stone Roses, T-Rex, Sex Pistols and the Small Faces. On its release as a single on October 10, 1994, it took the band to No. 7 in the UK charts.

The album version of 'Columbia' was upgraded from the original demo recording, and 'Bring It On Down' was

You and I are gonna live forever: 'Live Forever'.

the closest the band came to punk. 'Digsy's Dinner', 'Married With Children' (with Noel on vocals) and 'Sad Song' were a little more relaxed, moments of acoustic reflection written by an artist who has declared 'I'm a lover, not a fighter'.

Like 'Shakermaker' before it, *Definitely Maybe*'s eclecticism did give the record company's copyright people a few nervous moments: 'Digsy's Dinner' sports a riff that bears more than a passing resemblance to the Small Faces' 'Lazy Sunday', and 'Cigarettes And Alcohol' pays equal dues to T-Rex's 'Get it On'. Despite such fears, the album's reception was extraordinary. Even those not noted for liking rock — dance magazine *Mixmag*, for instance — applauded it: 'If you're into music,' concluded *Mixmag*, 'be it techno, hip hop, jungle or classic hands-towards-the-ceiling pumping house, you could still get into this.' Even the broadsheets, generally less responsive to hype and more critical with music reviews than the music press, lapped it up.

The one band that might have dented Oasis' sudden acclaim was the Stone Roses... had things turned out

Oasis stole indie pop's throne from Madchester pioneers the Stone Roses.

Noel strikes a pose for the 'Live Forever' video, recorded during Oasis' first Stateside trip.

differently. The great Manchester band that, arguably, saved British rock from oblivion in the late Eighties took five years to deliver their second album. The first was released in May 1989, their second — *The Second Coming* — in December 1994. The gap was crucial to Oasis, who might otherwise have looked as if they were merely copying the Stone Roses. When the Roses did return they were as aloof and cocksure as they'd always been, but they never had a chance of dethroning the Gallagher brothers.

It's weird being in a band with your **brother**. You go on **the road**, you **live** in the **same** van... we do **interviews together**. It's **hell**.

I live my life for the stars that shine: 'Rock'n'Roll Star'.

'Really it's just brotherly love,' says Peggy Gallagher about her battling sons.

Noel was well aware that their relatively late arrival on the Manchester music scene had made for a bigger struggle for acceptance. 'Someone said to us the other day that if it was 1987, we wouldn't even have to try. Two or three years ago at a local band night, everyone would go,' said Noel in July 1992. 'Anyone with a half decent tune was signed up,' he continued. 'If we'd been around in 1989, we would have been signed by now, but we would have been under serious pressure to deliver an album, but in eighteen months, we're going to be five times as good.'

He was right. By 1994, when the Stone Roses returned, Oasis were close to being the media phenomenon they are today. To promote *The Second Coming*, the Roses only did one interview, and that was a piece for the homeless

50

magazine, *The Big Issue*. It may have been a worthy gesture, but it was also evidence that the Roses had the same regard for the music press they always had. The album was slated.

Brotherly love

By contrast, Oasis were ever happy to talk to almost anyone, albeit that the real core of media interest was the relationship between Liam and Noel, the battling brothers Gallagher. With the arrival of 'Supersonic' much was made of Liam and Noel's unbrotherly love.

Their differences? Noel thought Liam had some growing up to do. Liam thought Noel was an overbearing know-it-all. This internecine battle was to keep the rest of the band in the shadows, where they have remained.

As teenagers in Burnage, Liam and Noel had to share a bedroom, something that Noel attributes to their bickering now. He reckons he got on all right with his elder brother, Paul, but had less time for Liam because he invaded his space. 'It's weird being in a band with your brother,' Noel told *The Observer* early in 1995. 'You go on the road, you live in the same van, then you go to your mam's for Sunday lunch and he's there. It's hell. Then we have to do interviews together and it all gets a bit much. We did an interview the other day and we actually agreed

on something. I think it was the fact that we were both in the same band.'

'Mam' thinks differently, of course. 'Really it's just brotherly love,' says Peggy Gallagher 'I think a lot of these wild stories are made up. They're not as bad as they're made out to be. Privately they've got great admiration for each other. Liam looks up to Noel because he writes the songs and Noel looks up to Liam because of his voice. They always look out for each other.

'When Liam used to come home from school, he used to be hyped up so much, he had that much energy, that he'd start on Paul and try to take the mickey,' she continues. 'Then he'd start on Noel, and Noel would just droop those eyebrows and that would be it. All that fighting stuff didn't really bother me at first. Why they argue so much is because they're in each other's company twenty-four hours a day. Every time Liam would leave here, I'd say to him, "Don't be fighting with Noel." Then Noel gets on the phone and says he never wants to talk to Liam again. What can you do?

'Liam was always a performer and liked to be the centre of things,' she says about her youngest son. 'He always stood out since he was a child and loved to be noticed. I suppose because Noel was a bit older than Liam, they don't always get on. Noel is the quieter one. Brothers often argue in families anyway.'

That much is true. But few arguments between brothers have been recorded and released *and* made the charts. An interview which took place between *NME* and Oasis on April 7, 1994 was released on vinyl and compact disc by indie label Fierce Panda. Released as *Wibbling Rivalry*, it reached No. 52 in the charts, the highest ever position for an interview record. At one point the interviewer suggested that the tension between the two brothers was what fuelled the band. Liam replied typically: 'Yeah. That's what it's all about. That's why we'll be the best band in the world, because I fuckin' hate that twat there. I fuckin' hate him. And I hope one day there's a release where I can smash fuck out of him, with a fuckin' Rickenbacker, right on his nose!'

If tension be the food of music, play on…

A **lot** of these wild **stories** are **made** up. **Privately** they've got **great admiration** for each other. **Liam** looks **up** to **Noel** because **he** writes the **songs** and **Noel** looks **up** to **Liam** because of his **voice.**

mrs gallagher

The brothers Gallagher.

definitely live forever maybe

A ugust and September 1994, Oasis embarked on a
short British tour to promote *Definitely Maybe*.
A fellow-traveller they took along was American
rock pin-up Evan Dando of the Lemonheads, who had
guested with them at their Virgin Megastore gig on the day
of the album's release. Dando performed an impromptu
acoustic support slot at the Buckley Tivoli on August 31, and
then at Manchester's Hacienda on September 5 he joined
supporting act Creation. The band that gave Alan McGee the
name for his label also had Andy Bell, from Ride, on guitar.

**I'm feeling Supersonic, give me gin
and tonic: 'Supersonic'.**

Dando wasn't the only rock star of rock that the
band met in September. Liam and Guigsy had an encounter
of the strange kind, be it more briefly, with the Who's Pete
Townshend. They spotted him in an airport lounge and were
suitably fazed because they'd just been reading about him
in a magazine. The situation turned out to be even more
macabre — Townshend happened to be reading a magazine
article about Oasis.

At the finish of the British tour, Oasis departed for
Japan on September 13. Over this six-date tour the band got
little sleep but collect plenty of presents from their Japanese
admirers. Feelings about Japan were mixed. Guigsy declared:
'I can't stand these groups who whine on about how tough
life on the road is. We love it — and we go for it.'

Lemonhead Evan Dando cuddling up to Noel during the *Definitely Maybe* tour.

After I've been to Japan for two days I want to go home. Everyone's too nice — no wonder Gary Lineker went there. There's **no** decent **food**, the **beer's** expensive, there's no **proper cigarettes**, you can't get **drugs**, and the **women** are **ugly.**

But Noel was always less enthusiastic. Commenting on the band's return trip a year later he says, 'After I've been to Japan for two days I start to get depressed and I want to go home. Everyone's too nice — no wonder Gary Lineker went there. The people get on my nerves. I just want to say, "stop bowing will you." There's no decent food out there, the beer's dead expensive, there's no proper cigarettes, you can't get drugs, and the women are ugly.'

For their part, the Japanese women needed no convincing about the merits of Oasis. As Daniela Soave reported in *GQ*, the band was attacked by an ear splitting shriek, louder than a wail of feedback, as hundreds of girls hurtled towards the tour bus. 'Oasis have provoked mass hysteria in the normally restrained Japanese fans,' she wrote, 'I could be witnessing the second coming.'

With the first Japanese tour out of the way, Oasis rested for only three days in Manchester before boarding a flight for the biggest test of any British band — their first

56

American tour. It would be a trip that would test their nerves to the limit.

The tour kicked off at Moe's in Seattle on September 23. Six days later they were at the Whiskey-A-Go-Go in Los Angeles, the Sunset Strip venue made (in)famous by the Doors and the Byrds in the Sixties. In LA, things began to hot up. On the day before, they were interviewed on alternative radio station KROQ. Liam's temper was tested as callers insisted on asking him about — of all things — scooters. 'Look, we're not fucking mods, alright?' he yelled at one caller.

Leaving the radio station, they went on to the Viper Room, film star Johnny Depp's famous night-spot and the place now hallowed by River Phoenix's tragic death. While it might be a popular Hollywood hang-out, it turned out to be less than friendly towards a bunch of Manchester blokes looking to sink a few. Following a fracas with the bouncers, an ejected Oasis returned to Bonehead's brother's house. Shortly after, the police arrived and cautioned Bonehead for disturbing the peace. It was said that he had been playing 'Supersonic' too loudly over and over into the early hours.

Next day, September 29, the Whiskey-A-Go-Go gig went badly. *NME* subsequently ran a piece titled 'Definitely Mayhem', highlighting the shambolic performance by Oasis and picking up on the tension between band and audience, which was reported to include Perry Farrell, Ringo Starr and celebrity DJ Rodney Bingenheimer. The set started with the bass amp blowing up. They were forced to start again. Second time around on the first song a crowd surfer was hurled against Liam's monitor speaker. This, coupled with a cameraman who kept distracting him, made him miss his vocal cues. He took his frustration out typically on Noel by slapping him on the back of the head with his tambourine. The crowd began chanting: 'Fight, fight, fight!'

After the gig the band had a 'heated chat' behind closed doors. Little was resolved, and things took a turn for the worse when Liam stormed out. Not to be upstaged, Noel left Los Angeles on a plane after informing the rest of the band the band that if they would not put in one hundred per cent, Oasis might as well split up and cancel the rest of the American tour. Fortunately, both Liam and Noel cooled down, and the rescheduled tour resumed.

Plenty of exposure

If America was a disaster, at least back home there was better news. 'Cigarettes And Alcohol', which had been released on October 10, gave them their highest UK chart position yet, reaching No. 7. Although not all critics were completely behind the band — 'They have as much chance of becoming the new Beatles as Danni Minogue had of becoming the new Diana Ross', wrote a *Daily Telegraph*

'...and the women are ugly,' says Noel about his Japanese fans.

writer — the public supported the record to a degree not usually afforded an indie band. Before Oasis, only Blur had received sufficient support to be considered an indie crossover band.

'Cigarettes And Alcohol' was more proof to anyone who needed it that Noel Gallagher could produce the ingredient most necessary in a successful pop song, a melody that deserved to be remembered. Like the singles that preceded it, this one was rich in catch phrases like: 'You gotta make it happen'. The three supporting tracks 'I Am The Walrus', 'Listen Up' and 'Fade Away' — were previously unreleased. The Beatles' 'I Am The Walrus', with which Oasis had ended their set when Alan McGee first saw

then in May, 1993, and which they have continued to use as their parting gesture, was recorded live at the Cathouse in Glasgow in June 1994. 'Listen Up' is another emotion-heavy rock ballad, and 'Fade Away' is an up-tempo number reminiscent of 'Rock'n'Roll Star'.

A higher chart position for 'Cigarettes And Alcohol' might have been achieved with the backing of a live *Top Of The Pops* appearance, but as the band were in America, viewers had to be content with a poor quality black and white video.

Their exposure was extended, however, when another new track appeared that month — an alternative recording of 'Bring It On Down' was given away on a

Oasis borrowed the Beatles' 'I Am The Walrus' to close their live set.

Oasis play the Virgin Megastore to plug the release of *Definitely Maybe*.

cassette that came free with *Vox* magazine. Also in October, Granada TV screened their *With Oasis* documentary, which contained footage from the Buckley Tivoli gig ('Digsy's Dinner' and 'Live Forever') and their Virgin Megastore show ('Shakermaker'), and was interspersed with chat from Liam and Noel.

Taking a step up

In America, Oasis played the Uptown Bar in Minneapolis on October 14. This time the gig went fine, but Liam came close to meeting a messy end from a gun-wielding American — an incident slightly more dangerous than the one Blur encountered, also on an American tour.

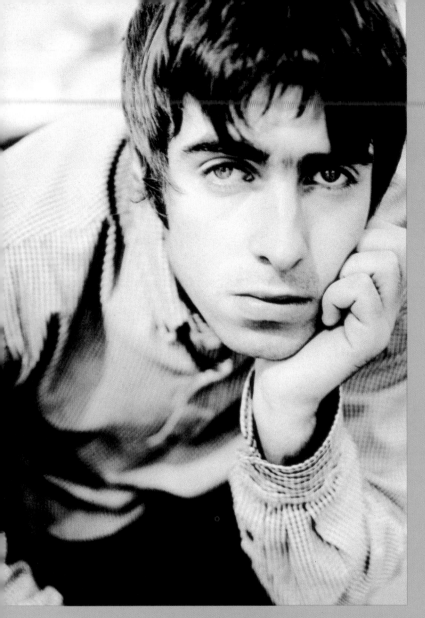

Liam adopts his 'why smile when a frown will do?' pose.

There was a toilet at the **back** of the **production** room and Liam kept **running** in and **out** of there practically the whole **night...** **bricking** himself.

'Bush were playing,' recalls Bonehead, 'and me and Liam went to see them, met them afterwards, ended up on a mad one, drank all their beer, ended up in some club, drank more beer, ended up somewhere else, drank more beer. It was like four in the morning, and we were staggering down this road. Some guy flies round the corner in a jeep, just misses Liam and Liam, being Liam's, like, "Here, watch it dickhead!" and starts shouting and screaming. Next thing we know the jeep stops and this geezer, this black guy about eighteen-stone, jumps out, pulls a gun out of his jacket pocket, and was like, "What did you say?"

'We're like blind drunk, I'm like that to Liam, "Liam, chill out." "No, I'll slap him, I'll slap him man, he can't

shoot me," and I was like that, "I bet he can."'

The closing gig of this first American tour took place at the New York Wetlands on October 29. All things considered, the tour had gone well, but they had failed to establish themselves as the Next Big British Thing; there was no Beatlemania for Oasis. They had merely followed in the footsteps of other great hopefuls: Frankie Goes To Hollywood, the Smiths, the Stone Roses, the Happy Mondays, Suede. In September *The Los Angeles Times* suggested that 'Oasis are just another perfectly gratifying but fairly mediocre pop outfit with fab sunglasses and mod hairdo'.

It took British music press writer Paul Lester of *Melody Maker* to sound a more optimistic note in October in the *Washington Post*. 'Traditionally, American bands are only ever any good at rock, while British groups are better at pop — and America doesn't really like pop,' he wrote, going on to say that Oasis were better placed in the USA than their counterparts, Blur, because their music lay between rock and pop.

From America, Oasis went to Europe, playing in France, Sweden, Germany, Holland and Belgium during November, before returning home in December. Their first British gig was at the Guildhall, Southampton. The size of the venues was going up, but Oasis habits remained the same, as Guildhall promoter Conal Dodds recalls: 'It was the first night of that tour and it was one step up, 1,800 people a night. There was a toilet at the back of the production room and Liam kept running in and out of there. He spent practically the whole night in the toilet bricking himself.'

A dude too many

As 1994 drew towards its close, Oasis could look back on it with some satisfaction. They had played just over a hundred gigs in twelve different countries, and the release of 'Whatever' on December 19 made their fifth commercial single in nine months. In keeping with the upward trend, it sold more than any of their previous single releases, and reached No. 3 in the UK charts.

The record wasn't without what was becoming another form of Oasis trend: possible copyright infringement. Nine days before its release, the band aired the song on the Jools Holland TV show, *Later*, and another artist accused them of ripping off one of his tunes. This time it was David Bowie. Bowie's lawyers suggested that Noel had nicked a bit from the Bowie-written Mott The Hoople song 'All The Young Dudes'. In the end 'Whatever' was released after Oasis agreed to remove the line causing most offence — 'all the young blues'.

The Oasis rhythm section, Guigsy and Alan, strolling on the streets of New York.

'Whatever' was held off the No. 1 position in the Christmas charts by the teenage rap sensation from London, East 17, and American subscriber to all things wholesome, Mariah Carey. The song is an epic. Eight minutes of Beatle-like vocal melody and string quartet arrangements (circa *Abbey Road*). It was the band's first recording since the *Definitely Maybe* sessions, and even by Oasis's standards it was a brave decision to release it just before Christmas when the charts usually become the domain of either old-timers or the latest teen sensations. Oasis were neither, yet they still sold 350,000 copies.

Melody Maker's Paul Lester described 'Whatever' as 'more like the Beatles than the Beatles'. Noel modestly described it as 'one of the best songs ever written', and on

With **every** song **that** I write, I compare it **to** the **Beatles.** I didn't start writing **songs** until I **was** about **fourteen,** so I just **used** to copy theirs.

'Twenty years ago maybe, but not now, he's just an old git,' says Noel after declining an offer to tour with Bowie.

the back of its success Creation Records began an advertising campaign that suggested Oasis were the 'International Guardians of Rock'n'Roll'.

Noel Gallagher had plenty to thank the Beatles for, and he has never ignored his debt. Bands like Queen, Jam and the Smiths had been influenced to different degrees by the Beatles, but for Oasis it was beginning to look like an obsession. They blatantly relied on Beatle sounds and imagery to capture a new market that neither knew nor cared about the Beatles, and an older market that could feel a nostalgia for the good old days of the Sixties.

The music press picked up on such comparisons early on in the band's career, but if music journos expected to score points from making the comparison obvious, they were to be disappointed. When asked, Noel frankly stated that the Beatles were 'of course, where I pinch all my songs from'.

'It's beyond an obsession,' concedes Noel about his passion for the four men who shaped international perceptions of pop music three decades before. 'It's an ideal for living. I don't even know how to justify it to myself. With every song that I write, I compare it to the Beatles. I didn't start writing songs until I was about fourteen,' he continues, 'so I just used to copy theirs.'

Beatling about

The Beatles had broken up when Noel was only four years old, and in the next ten years before he would begin writing songs, the most famous band ever of their time faded into little more than an interesting piece of history. It is probably fanciful, but nonetheless interesting to speculate that Noel Gallagher's anachronistic interest in his heroes owes something to the fact that he was born on the very day that the greatest of all Beatles' albums was released — *Sgt. Pepper's Lonely Hearts Club Band* — on May 29, 1967.

When Granada TV showed their Beatles tribute show, *All Together Now*, at the end of 1995, Noel offered this comment: 'If you look at our haircuts and the clothes we wear and even the guitars that I play and the amplifiers that I use… I mean, everybody always says to me, "You want to be Paul McCartney, don't you?" I went to [brother] Paul's house, and I had a brown suede jacket on and even he said, "You look like a Beatle." I spent an awful lot of money trying, so I should do.'

Noel's interest is clearly centred on the concept of 'Beatles' and the music the band achieved, not at all on the surviving personalities as they have grown up and away from the Beatles. About Paul McCartney (and other greats of the period) he says, 'Oh, he's lost it. They've all lost it.

The Beatles. 'An ideal for living', says Noel.

'They've been accused of being Beatle like, which is maybe the reason I like them,' reckons producer George Martin.

They've **all** lost **it**. **Ray** Davies, Pete **Townshend**, as songwriters, totally **lost it...** **People** hold John **Lennon** in esteem, **but** if he **hadn't** been **shot** how **sad** would he be **today?**

noel on history

Ray Davies, Pete Townshend, as songwriters, totally lost it... People hold John Lennon in this esteem, but if he hadn't been shot how sad would he be today?'

Reactions from rock's elder statesmen have been varied. 'They've been accused of being Beatle-like, which is maybe the reason I like them,' says George Martin, the producer of the Beatles who is often remembered as their fifth member. 'But they certainly show talent,' he adds.

George Harrison has always been less kind. 'Musically they're not bad, but we've heard it all before,' he says. 'The thing that worries me most are the comments they keep making on TV.'

The Beatles had generally been restrained in public about their favourite musical influences, and also a great deal more literate in their spoken comments, so Harrison's worries probably centre around statements like this from Liam, who shares his brother's fetish for all things Beatles: 'I don't reckon Elvis was the King, I reckon John Lennon

was. "Imagine" is one of the best songs ever. Totally. One of the scariest songs ever. Its just... "Imagine", innit? "Imagine", like, nish... or whatever.'

The extent of this Beatles fetishism extends beyond the music. Noel, who owns fifteen different recordings of

'I sort of feel there's a duty for us to educate everybody in this country under the age of twenty about music, of course that includes talking about the Beatles': Noel Gallagher.

'Strawberry Fields', makes sure that indicators are dropped all over the place. Johnny Hopkins, their PR man, recalls when he first met Oasis: 'The moment they walked into the room, you could feel the energy. It was just incredible, the way they joked around and responded to one another, it was exactly like when you see footage of the Beatles in America.'

No social issues

It was no coincidence that Oasis recorded 'Supersonic' and 'Shakermaker' at the studio made famous by the Beatles, Abbey Road. 'We had a choice of going to some place in Hackney or Abbey Road, so it was Abbey Road, no competition,' recalls Noel. 'We didn't do the zebra crossing thing, I think that's pretty stupid.'

Noel has always conceded that 'Supersonic' is his reply to 'I Am The Walrus', the song they close their live sets with. 'It's just a load of nonsense strung together. "I Am The Walrus" goes "semolina pilchard dripping from a dead dog's eye", and ours goes "I know a girl called Elsa she's into Alka Seltzer"'. Beatle fans were prone to attempt dissection of every nuance and hidden meaning in Beatle nonsense rhymes, so for Oasis scholars, according to Real People's Tony Griffiths, here is the reasoning behind Elsa: When Oasis were doing their three-day recording session at the Pink Museum, studio engineer Dave Scott's Rottweiler, who was called Elsa, used to fart all the time, and Noel kept saying she'd been filling up on Alka Seltzer.

Another Beatle reference can be found in the release date for the third Oasis single, 'Live Forever' — its August 8 release date was also the twenty-fifth anniversary of the *Abbey Road* LP. Look closely at the 'Live Forever' sleeve, and there you will find a photograph of the house where John Lennon grew up. 'I sort of feel there's a duty for us to educate everybody in this country under the age of twenty about music,' explains Noel. 'Of course that includes talking about the Beatles. How could it not? And, yeah, I don't mind people saying we've nicked riffs or lines or all sorts from them. Of course we do. Why not? They were the best, man.'

One Beatles' trait that Oasis didn't appear to share to any extent during 1994 was the need for social and

Musically they're not bad, but we've heard it all before. The thing that worries me the **most** are the **comments** they **keep** making on **TV.**

george harrison on oasis

political responsibility that Lennon had espoused. Although in 1995 Noel would align himself with the Labour party, he also suggested to MTV news that 'American youth are tired of people telling them how crap their lives are. I think when they listen to our records, we just tell them how good their lives could be'. There is an element of positivism in some of the songs — 'You and I are gonna live forever' ('Live Forever'), 'You gotta make it happen' ('Cigarettes And Alcohol'), and 'I'm free to do whatever I want' ('Whatever') — but this is hardly a match for the Beatles' 'All You Need Is Love', 'Let It Be' and 'Hey Jude' with the sentiment 'it's a fool who plays it cool and makes the world a little colder'.

Lennon was an egalitarian. The author of 'Imagine' financed student revolts of the late Sixties, went on anti-government marches and contributed to the political, spiritual and musical shaping of the world in his own way.

Liam Gallagher: the boys want to be him, the girls want to be with him.

'There's too many politically correct people knocking about for my liking,' responds Noel. 'If you write about social issues you're gonna get asked about them. Fortunately for us, we were writing about drinking, so we get asked about drinking.'

Brats' best band breaks hand

Oasis were hot at the beginning of 1995. Fuelled by the success of 'Whatever', and a string of sell-out UK gigs at the end of 1994, Noel spent the start of the new year writing a plethora of songs on his acoustic guitar, many of which appeared on the band's second album, *(What's The Story) Morning Glory?*.

Oasis spent some of January and all of February and March touring the USA and Canada, although they returned to Britain at intervals to record songs... and receive awards. On January 23, five days before playing DV8 in Seattle, Oasis (minus Bonehead, who was at home with his new-born baby, Lucy) attended *NME*'s Brats — the music paper's answer to the Brits. There they received awards for Best Band, Best New Band and Best Single for 'Live Forever'.

At this event tension in the indie camp was becoming evident as Oasis publicly slagged off others at the awards. Liam declared that all the other bands present weren't up to much, 'especially shit like Shed Seven.' But it was the rivalry between Oasis and Blur, which had been hotting up ever since the incident between Graham Coxon and Liam after Creation Records' tenth anniversary press conference, that was most obvious. The two bands sat at opposite ends of the room from each other, although on this occasion Liam and Noel kept their thoughts on the southern band untypically to themselves... not for long, though.

The winners of the Best Band award are chosen by *NME* readers, and as Noel collected the award, he said, 'You never really get to appreciate what you mean to your fans. Just a little tiny thing like them sticking a vote in a post-box, that means more to me than gold discs and the rest of it.' But later the same night at an after-show party at the Raw Club, the same trophy — shaped as a hand with its provocatively extended middle finger — was broken in some typically Oasis piece of mayhem.

After the awards Oasis announced a gig at the 12,000-capacity Sheffield Arena for April 22. It sold out within the same week and Oasis were in good spirits as they left for their intense two-month tour of the States. On February 18, after playing dates that took in San Francisco, Hollywood, Denver, Dallas and Memphis, Oasis finished the tour at the Masquerade in Atlanta, where according to a triumphant Liam 'the fans were hanging like bats from the ceiling'. Then it was back to Britain, and some recording time.

Determined not to let their UK chart success falter, Oasis arrived at the Loco studio in Wales on February 22, 1995 to record what would be their first No. 1 single, 'Some Might Say'; a song that Noel had written the previous summer. On his way to Wales, Noel's train became delayed and in a reported twenty minutes while waiting he

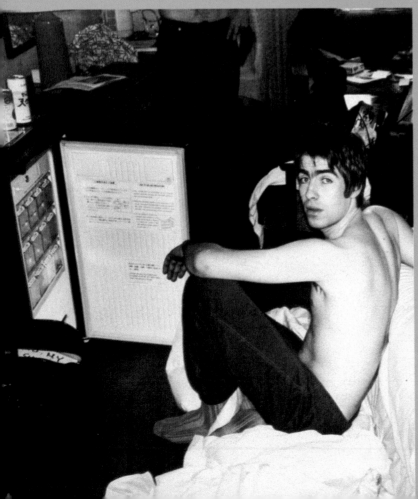

Half-clad Liam looking for refreshment.

I used to faint every time I had a spliff. The doctor said, "Basically you're alright with anything that gets you going, cos you need that." I love my doctor, man.

Even the stars suffer constipation.

managed to write 'Acquiesce', one of the supporting tracks for 'Some Might Say' — a song that demonstrates the intensity Noel is capable of when he delivers.

Billboard entry

Fresh from a fracas at Manchester's trendy watering hole, the Dry Bar (which was captured on security cameras and later broadcast on Channel 4's *The Word*), Liam arrived at the studio after Bonehead and Guigsy, who had already recorded their contributions in two days. Liam put his vocals down, and left Noel and producer Owen Morris the rest of the week to do the production.

Tuesday February 28, Oasis attended the British music industry's annual award ceremony, the Brits. Oasis were rewarded as the Best New Band, and fellow Manchester band, M-People, received the award for best dance act. But if the Brats had been Oasis' moment, the Brits was Blur's. The Essex band stole the show, winning four awards. Noel remained phlegmatic: 'Occasions like this are the pinnacle of music business pretentiousness, but I suppose it's all part of the job. It's good for a lig anyway.'

Before going back to the States, Noel visited his Harley Street doctor. 'Fucking Jason Donovan was in the waiting room,' he recalls. 'Now *he* needs to see a doctor. Smoking draw was my only problem cos I've got low blood pressure so I used to faint every time I had a spliff. The doctor said, "Basically you're alright with anything that gets you going, cos you need that."' He laughs. 'I love my doctor, man.'

On March 3, Oasis returned to the States, to play the Stone Pony in Ashbury Park, New Jersey. 'Live Forever' was at the top of the US college charts and *Definitely Maybe* had sold in excess of 220,000 copies, which put Oasis in the *Billboard* Top 75 album chart. The band was optimistic that they could improve on that by impressing audiences with the sixteen dates scheduled for the USA and Canada. They met tennis star John McEnroe at the Academy in New York (March 8), who turned up for the gig, and spent the night quizzing him about why he wasn't putting his own record out. The tour finished on March 25 at Milwaukee's Rave at Eagles.

This fragmented tour was a much greater success than the previous one. Most venues had sold out and radio stations across the country played tracks from

Definitely Maybe. Fans in their thousands turned up to watch, and hopefully meet the band, although to the bewilderment of audiences, Oasis did no encores, despite the applause. They also appeared on the *David Letterman Show*, 'the biggest chat show in the world' as Noel had been informed.

'We'd never fucking heard of it. But we're on our way to pretty big things out there,' he told *Q* magazine on his return to the UK. 'I hate the midwest though, I can't stand it. We sell a lot of records there and the people come to the gigs, but they don't seem to understand the band, they do all this moshing stuff to "Live Forever".'

Back in the UK, four days before playing the Cliffs Pavilion in Southend on April 22, Oasis made their first British TV appearance of the year, on the live-music show hosted by Mark Radcliffe, *The White Room*. Mark's show, *Hit The North*, had been the first to ever broadcast a live Oasis session, in July 1992, before they were

Ousted Oasis drummer Tony McCarroll.

Manchester dance band M-People, also winners at the Brits.

signed. On *The White Room* Noel joined with Paul Weller to play 'Talk Tonight'.

Drummed out

The pace of singles releases was beginning to tell, according to some music pundits. In reviewing the Cliffs Pavilion gig, *NME*'s Stuart Bailie pointed out that it was all very well to respect Noel for wanting to keep the band busy and releasing 'those epochal EPs every few months', but he had picked up signals from Southend that suggested Noel now required time to find songs to rival Blur. 'Basically,' he wrote 'they're gonna have to make it happen. All over again.'

Tensions from without spilled over into the band exacerbating a personality problem that had been festering for some time and came to a head on April 20, when Oasis

played the Bataclan in Paris. Liam and drummer Tony McCarroll had a stand-up fight in a hotel bar. The damage could not be repaired, and Tony's last appearance with Oasis was on *Top Of The Pops* on Thursday April 27, five days after the band's Sheffield Arena gig, three days after the release of 'Some Might Say'.

Relations between Tony McCarroll and the rest of the band had been faltering for over a year. Promoter at the Old Trout in Windsor, Phil Hanks, recalls an incident about a year earlier. 'They were already ignoring Tony McCarroll,' he says. 'They were playing football outside with the football on the radio really loud, it was "Everton vs Sheffield Wednesday". But no one would pass the ball to Tony. In the end, he was moaning so much someone just smashed the ball at him from about three feet away.' The previous September, when Noel was asked by an American caller to KROQ radio whether he had ever considered having a penis extension, Noel had replied that Oasis had one on drums and he didn't recommend it.

Tony was replaced by twenty-two-year-old Londoner and Charlton Athletic fan Alan White, the brother of Paul Weller's long-term percussionist, Steve White. 'On the Tuesday we sacked Tony, Tuesday night we didn't have a drummer,' recalls Noel. 'We were supposed to be doing *Top Of The Pops* the next night and everyone was going, "What have you done?" I sat there thinking, "Actually what have I done?"

'We were due to start the album that Friday,' he continues, 'and Tuesday afternoon I met Alan. So it suddenly dawned on me about five minutes before he was due to turn up, what if he's about thirty-two-stone? Anyway he came around the corner and I shook his hand and said, "You're in." And he went, "But don't you want to know what my musical influences are?" And I said, "No mate, you're under thirteen-stone, you'll do for me, you're in."'

Alan made his Oasis debut on *Top Of The Pops* on Thursday May 4.

Trashing the studio

A week after its release, their T-Rex ode, 'Some Might Say', reached No. 1 in the UK singles chart, knocking Take That's 'Never Forget' from that most prestigious of slots. Charged with the enthusiasm that a No. 1 record generates, Oasis entered Rockfield Studios, Wales, on May 8 to record the music for their next album. They remained there for just over a month.

Noel and Owen followed the pattern they'd established at previous sessions. They worked a long day, calling in the other members of Oasis to lay down their parts whenever they were needed. It was clear to all involved in its making that this second album was Noel's baby. He wrote the songs and he decided how they would sound when it came to mixing and producing them. He might have acted as the self-appointed chief but his behaviour could still be erratic. It was reported that 'Roll With It' took only one take to record, impressive considering Noel had returned to the studio that afternoon following a heavy drinking session, collapsed, and then had to be revived to record it.

Following the completion of six tracks, Liam, in celebratory mood, decided to invite a group of thirty people back to the studio from two local pubs. This prompted a big argument between the brothers.

'Me and Owen were working fifteen hours a day,' recalls Noel. 'Because the rest of them tended to put their stuff on last they tended to go down to the pub. But one night they brought half of south Wales back with them, and there was all these kids running around the grounds of the studio and all that, and somebody smashed a window in the studio and all the rest of it. It got a bit out of order.'

'He had a row with me about his ignorance towards people who he doesn't know,' says Liam, giving his version. 'He told someone to shut up and walk home because they asked him for a number for a taxi, and that person was my mate, and I said, "Don't talk to people like that who I know, just because you don't, because I'll just slap you." So we had a fight and that was it,' he says.

Glastonbury 1995.

Playing it their own way: Bon Jovi wanted Oasis to tour with him but Noel had other ideas.

We **turned** down **Bon Jovi** because it's **not** worth the **humiliation.** I **like** him **as** a **bloke,** but his group... **and** as for **Bowie,** twenty years **ago** maybe, but not **now.** He's **just** an old git.

noel on supporting

'And I trashed the place, yeah, because I went right off my tits.'

For the second time Noel left the band, issuing the ultimatum that if they weren't prepared to act like professionals then Oasis would have no future. He took a week off to stay with England and Blackburn Rovers' player Graham Le Saux in Jersey, and then returned to the studio feeling refreshed.

'They've split up twice on sessions that I've recorded with them,' recalls Owen Morris. 'And it's all about nothing, they always end up getting back together. Basically, the next day it's like nothing's happened, which is really weird. They love each other really.'

Maybe the last time

In the summer Oasis had a headline slot at the Glastonbury Festival on June 23, the same month they turned down David Bowie's offer to tour with him. They'd also previously turned down Bon Jovi and the Rolling Stones. 'We turned down Bon Jovi because it's not worth the humiliation,' says Noel. 'I like him as a bloke, but his group... and as for Bowie, twenty years ago maybe, but not now. He's just an old git.'

The night before Glastonbury, Oasis performed a warm-up (and low-key) gig at the Bath Pavilion, and spent some time during the day on the beach to shoot the cover for their next single, 'Roll With It'.

'Noel had a dream where he saw a load of televisions floating down a river, so he said, "Why don't we have TVs in it?" It was loosely based on the cover of *With The Beatles*,' recalls Microdot designer, Brian Cannon.

Liam and Robbie warm up for a gurning competition.

Glastonbury turned out to be something of a disappointment for Oasis. Because he had a cold, Noel spent the entire set wearing a duffle coat — the one he can be seen wearing on the cover of 'Roll With It' — and Liam took on the whole crowd when he challenged them to a scrap. Probably the most memorable incident was the arrival of Take That's Robbie Williams onstage with Oasis. Ex-Creation Records employee Tim Abotts recalls, 'That was the day Robbie left Take That. When Liam asked him onstage, that was his spiritual calling. The puppet strings were cut when he went offstage.'

To round off the evening the band got into a fight with rugby players. 'It all got messy,' Abotts remembers. 'It always follows the same route — "lines", Jack Daniels, punch-ups. They're the 7-Eleven of bands.'

After Glastonbury Oasis toured Europe, taking in Italy, France, Switzerland, Germany, Spain, Belgium and Ireland over July, except for July 14 and 15, when they played two Scottish dates on the beach at Irvine.

On July 25 it was announced that *(What's The Story) Morning Glory?* had at last been completed at Abbey Road studios. Expectations for this album ran high. Noel had already indicated to *NME* that he would only do one more album with Oasis and then call it a day. In the piece he was quoted as saying that there only so many anthems he could write. 'I don't know for sure but I'd say the next one will be the last one. I hope not, but that's the plan.'

Owen Morris told *NME* that he was astonished to hear Noel say this. 'It's the bollocks for this decade. It's a piece of piss recording with Oasis,' he said, and claimed that *(What's The Story) Morning Glory?* was more complete than *Definitely Maybe*. He finished by saying, 'It'll surprise a few people.'

Noel wrote most of the songs for *(What's The Story) Morning Glory?* on his acoustic guitar.

chained to the mirror

Oasis were twice losers in August 1995, to Portishead and, perhaps more importantly, to their old enemies, Blur.

Definitely Maybe was nominated for Best Album for the important Mercury Music Awards. Fellow nominees were Portishead for *Dummy*, Leftfield for *Leftism*, PJ Harvey for *To Bring You My Love*, Supergrass for *I Should Coco*, Tricky for *Maxinquaye* and Elastica for their eponymous album. Bookmakers William Hill gave Oasis odds of 3–1 on winning the £20,000-prize, the same odds it afforded Portishead, who were the eventual winners

'I'm just glad Blur aren't here,' said Noel at the event when quizzed for a response to losing.

But the Mercury awards were just a preliminary to another fight which the entire country's press came to dub 'The Battle of the Bands', when Blur brought forward the release of 'Country House' to August 14, the day advertised for the seventh single release from Oasis, 'Roll With It'.

It was a battle waiting to happen. There had already been plenty of bad blood in the recent past, and the situation had worsened when in May it was reported that Liam and Damon Albarn of Blur, almost came to blows over comments Liam made about Damon's girlfriend, Elastica's Justine Frischman. 'I gave it to her straight,' recalls Liam, 'told her Damon's an idiot. Then I said, "Come on, you and me, how about it? 'Girls who like boys and all that!'" But

Need a little time to wake up: 'Morning Glory'.

Portishead take the Mercury Music Award. Oasis don't.

They're just **middle** class ********, the Chas'n'Dave of pop. They're a **good comedy** band. Well, they make me **laugh anyway**. We're a proper band, I **always** knew **Oasis** would be the **next big** thing.

noel on blur

she just told me to get lost. I'll keep at her. I know it's happening. We fancy each other.'

For Albarn's part, he claimed that Noel had riled him at a party they both attended, when he claimed that Oasis' next single would prove what rubbish Blur really were. Blur's record company, Food, wouldn't admit to bringing the release date forwards to go head-to-head with Oasis, but it was just too good an opportunity to miss. It was like the Sixties all over again, when the Beatles (north) took on the Rolling Stones (south) in a battle to beat each other to the No. 1 slot on coincidental releases. The difference was that the Beatles and Stones, while public rivals remained private friends. Oasis and Blur were not, and the words began to fly.

'Blur bought their release date forward to coincide with ours,' claimed Noel angrily. 'They're just middle class bastards, the Chas'n'Dave of pop. I've heard their single and I think it's hilarious. They're a good comedy band. Well, they make me laugh anyway. We're a proper band, I always knew Oasis would be the next big thing.

'We'll go straight in at No. 1, without a doubt, with the single and our new album,' he stated on the day 'Roll

With It' was released. *(What's The Story) Morning Glory?* was scheduled for October 2.

Not only did the press have a field day as August 14 approached, so did the bookies, who made Oasis the favourites at 4–6, against Blur's 6–4. Just days after the release, it was clear that Blur were ahead of their northern rivals. 'We're selling about ten Blur singles for every nine Oasis,' said an HMV spokesperson that week. 'It's the closest race I have seen in a long time.'

'Come on, you and me, how about it? "Girls who like boys and all that",' says silver-tongued Liam to Damon's girlfriend, Justine Frischman.

Blur win the first battle, but not the war.

Don't let anybody get in your way: 'Roll With It'.

Although Oasis, not unsurprisingly outsold Blur in the north, the southern band made ground fastest, and Oasis lost the battle. A week after the joint releases Blur was at No. 1 and Oasis at No. 2. The last time that those both slots were taken simultaneously by new entries was 1989, when Jason Donovan's 'Sealed With A Kiss' was beaten to the top by Cliff Richard's 'The Best Of Me'.

'The main thing is that this is the seventh Oasis single in fifteen months and each one has sold more than

the last,' said Johnny Hopkins of Creation Records. 'That's a pretty amazing track record.'

Noel Gallagher wasn't so kind towards his record company. He believed a mix up with the bar codes on 'Roll With It' contributed to Oasis coming second. 'We've worked our bollocks off for that company and the biggest week in British pop history in thirty years and they weren't up to it,' he said about Creation.

But he reserved his bitterest scorn for Damon Albarn and Alex James. In an interview with *The Observer* he said that he had a lot of time for the guitarist and that he'd never met the drummer, but as to 'the bass player and the singer', he hoped the pair of them would catch AIDS and die because 'I fucking hate them two'.

Blur's offended record company pointed out that their band's worst verbal offence was to call Oasis Status

Three's company.

Quoasis. 'This is pathetic,' said Blur manager Andy Ross. 'Liam Gallagher has been banned from talking to the press as Noel is supposed to be the clever one speaking. Their capacity for saying stupid things is unbelievable.'

It was stupid and Noel, who was said to be drunk when he made the comment, knew it. He immediately expressed regret and publicly apologized to all who had taken offence and said he was 'horrified to find the journalist concerned chose to still run with it'. He continued by emphasizing his sympathy towards the plight of HIV carriers and AIDS sufferers, as well as being a supporter of raising awareness about AIDS. 'Although not being a fan of their music,' he concluded, 'I wish both Damon and Alex a long and healthy life.'

Although not being a fan of their music, I wish both Damon and Alex a long and healthy life.

Noel on Blur (again)

Noel with his two favourite Pauls (and Johnny Depp).

As a coda to his retraction, Oasis later recorded a version of 'Hey, You've Got To Hide Your Love Away' for World Aids Day. The track was played on Radio 1 but never released.

In one important sense both bands won the battle. The media feeding frenzy gave enormous exposure to indie music, and almost overnight the previously obscured Britpop scene had been turned into a national currency. Both bands were now the property of the public, and much wealthier for it. Music industry analysts suggested that over seven days more than one million pounds was dished out by fans on both records. 'They put a lot of emphasis on their chart position, although the album sales actually count for more,' said an EMI spokesperson once the result was known. In the first week 'Country House' sold 280,000 copies, 'Roll With It' 250,000. The Blur CD was priced £1 lower.

Guigsy goes

At the end of August, following a seven-date Japanese tour, Oasis returned to the UK and Noel was invited to contribute to the Bosnia *Help* album. He recorded 'Fade

And then there were four. When the other Manchester boy band lose Robbie Williams some fans merely blame Oasis, others spit at them.

Away' on September 5, at the Abbey Road studios under the heading of Noel Gallagher And Friends. Johnny Depp played guitar on this track and Lisa Moorish provided the vocals. Noel also played rhythm guitar for The Mojo Filter's version of 'Come Together', alongside Paul Weller and Paul McCartney.

Having said little complimentary about the ageing Beatle, Noel says now that working with Paul McCartney was better than talking to him. 'I've not really got a lot to say to him. I never learned "Come Together", and he showed me the chords. I said, "It's a piece of cake, this."'

In September Oasis were also approached to write a song for the England Football Club. 'Over my dead body, we're Irish,' exclaimed Noel. 'Let Blur do it, they're English,' said Noel. And Bonehead got married to his childhood sweetheart, Kate.

You can't afford to even have six months off, because you come back and someone's invented another scene, and suddenly you're old hat.

noel

Guigsy had become exhausted and left the band suddenly, to be replaced by Scott Mcleod.

Otherwise September turned out poorly. Early in the month they pulled out of a Bournemouth show after Blur booked a gig in the town for the same night. Police feared the football-like rivalry between the two band's supporters could escalate into a full-scale battle. And supporters of another British pop band also expressed a dislike for Oasis. Fans of Take That, who reckoned that Oasis were responsible for Robbie Williams leaving the group, spat at Liam as he arrived at Manchester airport.

Next, they were forced to reschedule their UK and European tour through September when Paul McGuigan suddenly left the band, citing nervous exhaustion.

Bassist Scott McLeod got his 'fifteen minutes' while Guigsy had a break.

Noel, who had been only too happy to see drummer Tony McCarroll leave in April, was adamant that Oasis couldn't cope without Guigsy on bass. 'Paul is Oasis,' said Noel after the departure. 'If he leaves, the band is finished. It's that simple. Paul is tired and exhausted. He's decided he's not in a right physical condition to go on so we told him to have a holiday. It's meant we've had to cancel a few shows, but he's a mate and that comes first.'

Oasis needed a bassist, especially with further USA tour dates set, so a replacement was found in Scott McLeod of Manchester band the Ya Yas. He was asked to fill in for six months, the period of rest Guigsy's doctor recommended. Before making this decision, McLeod asked the advice of Ya Yas' manager, Gareth Evans, who'd previously managed the Stone Roses. 'I told him, in the strongest possible terms, to join,' recalls Gareth.

If we **were** to take John Lennon, Jimi Hendrix, Ray Davies, Steve Marriot — anybody's **first** two **albums** against my first **two** albums — I'm **there** with the **Beatles.**

noel on modesty

Less then two weeks later, out came *(What's The Story) Morning Glory?*. The release celebration was, however, inglorious. Oasis planned to play a midnight acoustic gig at Tower Records in London's Piccadilly Circus. But having spent all afternoon watching Liverpool vs Manchester United in a Camden Town pub, Noel arrived at Tower Records to find the band in an even more inebriated than he was.

**Temporary bassist Scott McLeod 'does one'
during an American tour...but he didn't
do it for very long.**

All your dreams are made, when you're chained to your mirror with your razor blade: 'Morning Glory'.

A new maturity

(What's The Story) Morning Glory? took Oasis to new heights. The album that had already spawned two big hits — 'Some Might Say' and 'Roll With It' — entered the UK album charts at No. 1. It sold 350,000 copies in its first week, and pushed Blur's fourth album, *The Great Escape*, to No. 5. Noel was very confident. 'If we were to sit down now and take John Lennon, Jimi Hendrix, Ray Davies, Steve Marriot — anybody's first two albums against my first two albums — I'm there, I'm with the Beatles.'

The record buying public seemed to think so, too. *(What's The Story) Morning Glory?* became the fastest-

selling album since the release of Michael Jackson's *BAD*. 'This new one has sold more in a day than Blur sold in a week. It's been astonishing,' said that ever-impartial HMV spokesperson in the first week of sale.

Alongside Take That, Simply Red, Black Grape and M-People, Oasis were another success story from Manchester. The city was so enamoured with the cultural and financial power its bands wielded that Labour and Liberal Democrat councillors put forward a motion to congratulate all these bands on their 'spectacular chart success'.

'I think the sound of *Definitely Maybe* was a bit one dimensional,' Noel Gallagher told *NME*, but he thought there was a lot more variety in the new songs and a lot more going on.

There certainly was, *What's The Story?* was galvanic. Again Oasis had managed to borrow sounds popularized by the Stones, T. Rex, the Kinks, the Small Faces and, especially, the Beatles, without losing their own charismatic identity. This album confirmed Oasis were a band with two song types. Their R&B anthems of masculinity — 'Hello', 'Roll With It' — and their slower, wistful, not-quite love songs — 'Don't Look Back in Anger', 'Cast No Shadow'.

Earls Court played host to Oasis, the biggest ever indoor show staged in Europe...

...where they entertained 20,000 a night.

Bonehead plays a G for the fans at Earls court.

If *Definitely Maybe* was about the band's desire to transcend the mundane, *What's The Story?* is a cooling down of that bravado, as in Noel Gallagher's quest for self discovery — 'Champagne Supernova' — and his expression of sensitivity — 'Wonderwall'.

Most of these songs were written on an acoustic guitar first and the result is less harsh, the chords are more full. And Liam's voice changed to accommodate that. The nasal, heavy tone that posed all over *Definitely Maybe*, occupying territory somewhere between John Lennon and John Lydon, became a warm, almost vulnerable lilt for *What's The Story?* In 'Wonderwall', 'Don't Look Back in Anger' and 'Cast No Shadow' Oasis might have discovered something that could be considered their feminine side — but they still rock. 'Hello', with its Gary Glitter Chorus lifted verbatim from the original, 'Some Might Say' and 'She's Electric' revel in Oasis' harder influences.

There are Beatles references all over: 'Wonderwall' is the name of a George Harrison album, there are instrumental breaks reminiscent of the one that closes 'Strawberry Fields', 'Morning Glory' drops a Beatles' song

Earls Court goes 'mad for it'.

Bonehead plays a G for the fans at Earls court.

title with the line 'Tomorrow never knows what it doesn't know too soon', and 'Don't Look Back In Anger' borrows the opening bits of 'Imagine'.

The drugs references are there as well. 'Morning Glory' offers the line 'All your dreams are made when you're chained to the mirror and the razor blade'. And 'Champagne Supernova' asks 'Where were you when we were getting high?'

On the vinyl version of *(What's The Story) Morning Glory?*, there is an additional track, 'Bonehead's Bank Holiday'. Written by Noel, it features Bonehead on vocals. A track that had been selected for the album but had to be removed was 'Step Out'. It sounded so much like Stevie Wonder's 'Uptight' that he reportedly demanded six per cent royalties from the entire album.

Stevie Wonder must have known he would be onto a good thing. Such was the reaction to *(What's The Story) Morning Glory?* that by early 1996 it had sold over two million copies in the UK, gone Top 10 in every major European country, and was a No. 1 in Australia. Blur might

Manchester bored me because it's too small. You can't fart without everybody knowing about it.

noel

have won the singles battle but Oasis had won the war. According to Alan McGee of Creation Records, Oasis' real competition was 'U2 and the Beatles' back catalogue'.

Guigsy returns

Oasis were back in the USA on October 7, with their temporary bassist, Scott McLeod. He proved to be very temporary — on October 17 he walked out after a show in Buffalo, New York, and returned to England.

'He comes offstage and went straight to bed on the tour bus,' recalls Noel about the events surrounding Scott's

Liam coated up for the Earls Court gig.

Mike Flowers Pop had more success with 'Wonderwall' than Oasis. Noel reckoned it was the sign of a great song.

departure. 'Anyway, the bus takes off and the tour manager has this look on her face and we went, "What's up with you?" And she went, "Well, I've got some bad news... Scott's just said he wanted to go home."' Noel decided to let Scott sleep on it. 'If he got up in the morning and changed his mind fair enough. By the time we got up in the morning he was on the plane home.'

It was bad news. Oasis had a tour to complete and were scheduled to appear on the most popular chat show in the US, the *Late Show* with David Letterman, within a couple of days. They managed one gig, but as a four-piece, with Bonehead on bass. McLeod had left confusion in his wake.

'Funny thing is, he didn't speak to me personally about it until I got back from America,' says Noel. 'He phoned up... and he said, "Alright, it's Scott," and I went, "Well, what do you want?" And he's actually changed his mind, he said, "Oh, I think I've made the wrong decision." And I said, "Yeah well, I think you have, and good luck with signing on."'

The band returned to Britain in disarray, with two sell-out nights at the Earls Court Exhibition Centre looming and no bass player. Noel had little choice but to put pressure on the still-frail Guigsy. He was reluctant, but Noel's arguments proved persuasive and he returned. The Earls Court gigs, November 4 and 5, were another triumph for Oasis.

'They were the best gigs I've ever done in my life,' recalls Noel. 'I had to sit down and have a drink to comprehend it. The fans confound me. Both albums have sold over 900,000 now. I mean, I meet these kids in the street and they're shaking but I'm saying: "I'm honoured to meet you."'

After the Saturday night show Noel presented each member of the band with a scooter — a touch of irony which would probably be lost on American radio show phone callers. The Sunday night support band, the Bootleg Beatles, were presented with a jeroboam of champagne and the pithy comment: 'I really wanted the Beatles to support

but they couldn't make it. Besides I hate every other band in the country.'

The Earls Court shows were the largest indoor music events ever staged in Europe, and absolute proof that public support for Oasis had made them into the heavyweight champions, despite poor critical reviews for *(What's The Story) Morning Glory?*.

Make it chocolate-brown

Before the album's release, media fall-out from the Battle of the Bands was concluding that Oasis weren't worth the hype. After all, they'd lost to Blur. Plenty of the pundits were less than complimentary of *(What's The Story) Morning Glory?*. *Q* magazine suggested that it balked 'at most of the hurdles facing it, seemingly content to re-iterate certain basic points from *Definitely Maybe*'.

And tonight, on lead guitar and backing vocals...

The reviewer considered it was unlikely that Noel or the band had peaked and that it was time for a musical rethink.

Oasis fans didn't agree, they bought 350,000 copies in the first week of sale, and on the Monday after the Earls Court gigs, 'Wonderwall', the third song to be pulled from the second album as a single, went into the UK charts at No. 2. 'Wonderwall' stayed in the charts for so long that the release of follow-up single 'Don't Look Back In Anger' had to be delayed until the middle of February 1996. Its chart success was also influenced by the Mike Flowers Pops, who released an easy-listening version after the original had peaked. The popularity of this reworking was such that it kept the original in the charts for much longer than might ordinarily have been the case. In the end the Mike Flowers Pops cover lost pole position to Michael Jackson's 'Earth Song'.

'When I first heard that someone had done a cover of "Wonderwall", I was like... well, who? I'd never heard of him,' recalls Noel. 'But when we got the tape, we fell about in hysterics, but not in a derogatory way, everybody in the band thought it was great. It's a great song, the way we do it. But he's changed all the chords round and kept the same melody, and that is the sign of a great song. I'd like to hear anybody doing a Nine Inch Nails cover.'

Early in December 1995, Oasis returned to the US to play the dates rescheduled by Scott McLeod's leaving, with a recovering Guigsy on bass. Here they received the news they'd been waiting for: 'Wonderwall' had entered the *Billboard* charts at No. 21, *Definitely Maybe* had now sold in excess of half a million copies and, more importantly, *(What's The Story) Morning Glory?* had sold 1.2 million copies in America alone.

After playing the last US date of 1995 on December 18, the band flew back to London, where Creation threw a party in their honour at the Halcyon Hotel in Holland Park. At midnight Alan McGee thanked Oasis for Creation's most successful year and awarded them with presents. Alan White received a cheque to cover the cost of a new Mini Cooper he'd just bought, Bonehead got a Rolex, Guigsy

I kept thinking, I hope if I ever met so-and-so that he's not a **prat,** because it would **shatter** my **illusions.** When I did meet these people they were **dead** normal. And that's **how** I am, too.

Liam at the MTV Awards, November 1995.

membership of a gym and Liam a guitar. It didn't look like there was anything for Noel.

'All the bands were getting boxes with presents in, and I'm thinking there's nothing there with my name on, this is bang out of order,' recalls Noel. At this point Alan McGee ushered Noel outside and pointed at a parked car — a chocolate-brown Rolls-Royce Corniche.

'It was the first time I've ever seen the guy completely dumbfounded,' recalls Alan McGee.

Not quite. Noel responded, 'But what am I supposed to do with it? I can't drive.'

1995 had been a monster year for Oasis. Their first No. 1 single, the battle with Blur, and the success of their second album (at home and abroad) had made them a household name. Oasis took the front cover of practically every magazine dedicated to music and lifestyles during the year, not to mention the tabloid interest in them. This success didn't appear to make Noel complacent. In a rare moment of humility Noel told *Q* magazine that Oasis weren't necessarily the best band around but they were certainly the biggest.

McCarroll's revenge

To remain the biggest band could only be achieved through hard work. Talking to Manchester's *City Life* magazine at the close of 1995, Noel told music writer Chris Sharratt that 'the reason we never stop is because we don't want to.'

'For a long time bands have got to a certain level and taken two years off, and then think they can just waltz back in again and pick up where they started,' he said in December 1995. 'But music moves so fast these days you can't afford to even have six months off, because you come back and someone's invented another scene, and suddenly you're old hat.'

1995 was also the year that Noel left Burnage for Camden Town, London. 'People have got this thing about me being anti-Manchester,' he says defensively. 'But I don't know where that one came from. I go back to Manchester a lot, it's just that I don't go to the Dry Bar or the Hacienda, or try to get into clubs on the guest list. I go and see my mam, stay at some hotel and then go back to London. Manchester bored me because it's too small. You can't fart without everybody knowing about it. At least in London you've got other famous people, like the Queen and that.

'It's good at the moment because everything we touch turns to gold,' he continues. 'We put on a gig and it's sold out before you can say, "What time's the box office open?" But if there's one reason why we carry on doing these things it's because one day everything we touch is going to turn to dog

With amazing grace Oasis accept three awards at the Brits, February 1996.

> People ask my **advice** about a lot of things. I'm **good** at giving it but **not** at taking it. But people like **Paul Weller** will look after me, they'll make **sure** I'm **conscious** in a chair or that I can get **home.**
>
> *noel on friends*

shite, and we're not going to be able to do these massive gigs, so we might as well enjoy it while it's here. It can all change very quickly. It can't last forever.'

It was still looking good for Oasis at the start of 1996, though. *(What's The Story) Morning Glory?* climbed to No. 5 in the *Billboard* US album chart, and both versions of 'Wonderwall' were being heavily rotated (every half hour) by influential music channel MTV.

In January Oasis played four dates in Germany, then returned to play their first British gig of the year at the Whitely Bay Ice Rink in Tyne & Wear, their first show in the north-east since August 1994 when Noel had been attacked (with the exception of a snooker ball discovered onstage afterwards, the show went well).

To dent this roll of good fortune, ousted drummer Tony McCarroll announced his intention to sue Oasis in January. His legal representatives claimed that he had been improperly forced out of the band in April the previous year. 'Mr McCarroll believes his expulsion arose from personal differences between himself and Noel Gallagher — something he claims had nothing to do with his abilities as a musician. Therefore, he concludes, his removal was unlawful.'

Along with the rest of the band, McCarroll had signed a contract at the end of 1993 with Creation that made him an equal partner, entitling him to a one-fifth share of the band's recording royalties, As the songwriter, Noel was to receive a hundred per cent of the publishing royalties. The writ McCarroll's solicitors issued claimed damages for their client because he'd been excluded from recording the drum parts for (What's The Story) Morning Glory?.

And yet more awards

In February Oasis put tickets on sale for their end-of-April gig at the Manchester City's ground, Maine Road. Forty thousand tickets sold within two hours, breaking all previous records. A second show was hastily announced and also sold out in record time.

Citations were still coming Oasis' way. At the NME Brats the previous year Oasis had won three awards. This time Noel accepted four on behalf of the band: Best Band, Best Single, Best Album and Best Live Band. In fine Oasis style, he offered this comment before leaving the stage: 'It's hard to be humble at a time like this, so I won't try. You're all shit.'

At the Brits Oasis received three awards: Best Band, Best Album and Best Video for 'Wonderwall'. The 1996 Brits were an occasion of controversy for several reasons, and

> It's about **looking forward** rather than looking **back. I hate people** who look back on the **past** or **talk** about what **might** have **been.**
>
> **noel on don't look back**

Oasis ensured their part would also be remembered. They started winding up the organizers by refusing to play live at the venue for the event — their old stomping ground Earls Court — suggesting instead that they play the approach, an opportunity for their fans, as well as the gathered glitterati of the music business, to see them live. The organizers refused.

When it came to the awards, Liam demonstrated what value they had for him by attempting to insert one up his rear end. He also had a crack at Michael Hutchence who presented Oasis with an award, asking him for a fight. Then he led Oasis in their version of Blur's 'Parklife', which had the chorus 'Shitelife'. To round off, Noel suggested to the audience, which included Tory minister Virginia Bottomley, that they all vote Labour.

Commenting afterwards Noel asked, 'Why was Michael Jackson there, apart from furthering his career? And that fat idiot from Simply Red, what was he doing with 650,000 dancers onstage?'

Only two albums into their recording career, Oasis were attracting famous people to them, just as the Beatles had done before them. Former Take That member,

Robbie Williams, described them as a 'top people's band'. At the Mercury Music awards in August 1995 Labour party leader Tony Blair told Noel that he played his album every morning in the car, to which Noel replied that when Labour took office they should sort out the education system. When Liam celebrated his twenty-third birthday a party was thrown in his honour by Paula Yates and Michael Hutchence at record producer Nelee Hooper's London flat. Another celebrity couple won over to the Oasis cause were film star Johnny Depp and his girlfriend, model Kate Moss.

Their gigs have also attracted plenty of the rich and famous. George Michael, Jason Orange (another former member of Take That), Amanda Donohoe, Bono, The Edge, and Adam Clayton of U2, Janet Jackson and Ringo Starr have been guest-listed for many of their shows. Metallica drummer Lars Ulrich spent a large portion of 1995 with the band, until he was eventually thrown off the tour bus for being a pest.

Friends and centrefolds

Oasis were also in good company when they contributed designs for greetings cards for Help, the initiative to help children suffering from the blood bath of Bosnia. Fellow contributors included David Bowie, the Boo Radleys, Iggy Pop, Peter Gabriel, Thom Yorke of Radiohead, Kate Bush, Dave Stewart, Brian Eno and Jarvis Cocker from Pulp.

Of course, the press is generally more interested in the seamier associations — a preoccupation with Liam's sexual encounters, for instance. The women that Liam has been associated with include solo singer Lisa Moorish and Berri, Amanda De Cadanet, Helena Christensen, actress Kadamba Simmons, and film star Patsy Kensit — 'We're perfect for each other, we both love getting off our heads,' says Liam about his relationship with Patsy. Such is the interest in them that *For Women* magazine offered Liam and

Game-on.

Noel £100,000 to star as nude centrefolds. 'We wanted to feature them because they are sexy in a rough and ready way,' said editor Ruth Corbett.

'I think it was something that was just waiting to happen and we were just a catalyst for bringing a lot of people together,' says Noel about the lifestyle he leads that would be a shocker to the working-class lads he knocked about with five years before. 'I like having lots of friends, as long as they don't expect me to be anything other than me. I'm always up for being myself, I think people expect artists to be aloof and sullen, but I think when people meet me they are quite surprised because I'm not much like that. I'm up for a chat and I'd much rather talk about *Coronation Street* or *Eastenders* than Oasis and our music.

'When I first met Paul McCartney, I said, "How's it going?" He said, "can't complain." And I thought, no,

Is it really you? enquires Paula Yates.

I bet you can't with four-hundred million quid in the bank,' recalls Noel. 'What a stupid question. What's he going to say to that? "Oh, I'm down to my last two-hundred million and I'm feeling a bit skint actually." But it has restored my faith in musicians. I kept thinking, I hope if I ever met so-and-so that he's not a prat, because it would shatter my illusions. When I did meet these people they were dead normal. And that's how I am, too.'

'Oasis haven't got a pop star attitude,' says Creation's Johnny Hopkins. 'There's an honesty there, the music and the look are real. All the girls want to shag them and all the boys want to be in the group. They fulfil people's dreams.'

Fame for the band members is one thing, it isn't always as exciting for the families. 'I'm getting fed up being chased around by these females,' says Paul Gallagher. 'Most of them couldn't give a damn about me — they just want to use me to get to Noel and Liam. At the moment I'm being stalked by a mad Oasis fan. She's knocked at my house twice and asked my mam if I've got a girlfriend. I've had some pretty blatant offers but they're just fanatical teenagers and I've never taken advantage of them. They tell you how great you are and how much they love you. But they're nutters. I just tell all of them to get lost — no matter how gorgeous they are.'

Our kid doesn't sing

Delayed by the success of 'Wonderwall', the fourth single to come from the second album was released on February 9. 'Don't Look Back In Anger' went straight in at No. 1 in the UK charts. In a gesture of recognition that Oasis were now truly top of the pops, the TV show of the same name allowed them the rare privilege of playing two songs on the show, an accolade previously only afforded to the Beatles and the Jam. After the single, Oasis played their cover of the Slade song, 'Cum On Feel The Noize'.

'Don't Look Back In Anger' sparked another bout of internecine Gallagher warfare. It was the first Oasis single in which Noel took the vocals, and whenever it was played live, Liam usually walked offstage.

The fans confound me. I mean, I meet these kids in the street and they're shaking but I'm saying: "I'm honoured to meet you."

noel

'I'd written these two songs for the LP, "Don't Look Back In Anger" and "Wonderwall",' says Noel about his vocal role. 'I wanted to sing "Wonderwall" because the guitars are acoustic, but our kid insisted that he wanted to sing it. So I said, alright, but I'm gonna do "Don't Look Back In Anger" then, and it's going to be a single at Christmas, and you won't be singing on it. I think he thought I was bluffing.'

Noel responds firmly to the suggestion that he might feel sorry for putting Liam in such a position. 'No, I do not. He made his choice, simple as that. I'm twenty-eight, he's twenty-three. I don't want to argue with him no more. I don't feel sorry for anyone. No. Why should I? It's not as if he's got a bad life, is it?'

best band in the world

'With saying we were going to be bigger than the Beatles, we're in a position where it could go one way or the other. We have to put up or shut up — and we've never been ones for shutting up,' says Noel Gallagher about his lust for a life in which Oasis are the biggest rock band in the world. At the time of writing they certainly are in Britain, and their reception in Europe, Australia and Japan is no less enthusiastic.

America though, that's a harder nut to crack for a British band. Plenty have succeeded elsewhere but died a death in the US: Suede, Blur, the Smiths, the Jam, the

A penny for them...

Stone Roses and the Happy Mondays. Richard Griffiths, head of Oasis' US record label, Epic, attributes this relative lack of success to complacency. 'Americans have generally had better bands over the last few years,' he explains. 'Hyped British groups came over, did ten shows in places like Los Angeles and New York, grudgingly went to the radio stations and slagged the DJs off, flew back to Surbiton and thought everyone in America was going to fall at their feet, which was absolute rubbish.'

In support of this sentiment, U2's manager, Paul McGuinness, observed in 1992, 'There is normally a generation of English groups going through the American system at almost every level, but it didn't happen this time. The bubble seems to have burst.'

In recent times it has only been stadium players, like

Everyone's having too **good** a time to be **bothered** going on holiday for **six** months, that's **boring** man.

noel on relaxation

U2 and Depeche Mode, who have sustained success in the States, and such leftfield bands as Bush — who, to date, have sold over three million of their grunge-influenced album, *Sixteen Stone* — Elastica, Portishead and Everything But The Girl are beginning to score solid sales in the US.

But Oasis wanted more than solid sales. They wanted to be massive everywhere, and that definitely included America. One of the earliest signs that this aspiration might be accommodated was given when eight of America's top radio executives arrived at the Hurlington Club in London. There, they listened to tracks by Blur, Supergrass, Pulp, Black Grape and Oasis. Some they would choose to play on their stations, ones that were capable of breaking bands in America. Their favourite was the title song from *(What's The Story) Morning Glory?*. The second choice was 'Kelly's Heroes' by Black Grape. 'The Universal' by Blur and 'Common People' by Pulp were considered 'too English'.

On February 22, 1996, Oasis embarked upon their sixth American visit, where they played Kansas City, Missouri. The venues on this tour were stadiums, each with

John Lennon 1970. Sorry, Liam Gallagher 1995.

American exposure for Oasis on the *David Letterman Show*, January 1996.

a capacity of between three and four thousand. This was a pivotal moment for Oasis. *(What's The Story) Morning Glory?* had been in the *Billboard* chart's Top 5 for three weeks, radio and TV rotation of 'Wonderwall' was intense, and the tour was a sell-out. The excitement left many commentators concluding that Oasis were arriving in the same fashion as did the Beatles in 1964. At the time of writing it has yet to happen. But that doesn't mean it won't.

It is worth looking at the band's relationship with America.

Oasis chill backstage in Berkeley.

Oasis have things against them. They're a rock band who are static live, they adopt none of the conventional rock posturing, or the sloganeering between songs, that American audiences like. And they don't tolerate stage invasions. On occasions Liam has threatened stage divers, 'Any of you touch me, an' you'll get a smack'.

They are also indisputably British, which always meant being greeted by initial cynicism in the American press. 'I gather that the UK looks upon Oasis as archetypal bad boys, but over here they're seen like wimp troubadours,' said America rock critic Gavin Edwards. 'So Liam and Noel get into schoolboy tussles every now and then? Please. In America, stars such as Snoop Doggy Dogg stands trial for murder, and then write songs about it. At best, the Gallagher brothers' scrapes give them the aura of plucky Dickensian chimney sweeps'

The Chicago Sun-Times was kinder. It called Oasis 'glorious', describing Liam's voice as 'at once monotonal and alluring', but it did suggest that Bonehead, Alan White and Guigsy were little more than hired hands, that they were like 'background extras in someone else's movie'.

They are also indisputably British sounding. A problem the band still encounters is that Americans find it hard to understand their accents, let alone their grip on the ironic. 'I've seen a piece on MTV news where they actually put subtitles up on the Gallaghers because they couldn't understand their accents,' recalls Griffiths. At the close of 1995 Stuart White, who wrote his USA Diary for *News Of The World*, told his readers that Oasis were getting the American press interested, but they were having a problem getting their heads around phrases like 'I'm double mad for it' and 'We're Top Drawer'.

As in Britain, the US authorities also took an interest in the band that at times threatened to dent their career. As the band embarked on their sixth US tour rumours were rife that being 'known' as having a fancy for Class A drugs could have them kicked out of the States. 'They sound like trouble. We'll be glad to see the back of them,' said a New York Police spokesperson.

'It's all a lot of nonsense,' retorted Paul Gallagher. 'People are saying all kinds of daft things. This sounds like sour grapes to me — probably a rival record company trying to stir up trouble deliberately. The lads have no convictions for drug taking and they know full well the situation with drugs over there. Their management certainly do. There won't be any bother.'

Strategic attack

Oasis, of course, have plenty going for them, too. They have been able to win over the American psyche gradually by having caught music fans in a flux brought on by the breakdown of the alternative music scene. Early in 1996 queen of grunge Courtney Love told subscribers to her post-grunge grunge to boycott Oasis gigs. 'Oasis must die. Do not buy Oasis records. They come to rape and pillage our women and invade America,' was the message she posted over the internet.

An enormous strength of the band is their blatant desire to realize their 'best band in the world' boasts by breaking the US big time. 'They unashamedly want to be successful at a time when a lot of American bands have been quite deliberately doing what they can to try and limit their success and be very much the anti-hero,' says Griffiths about Oasis. 'The Gallagher brothers have shaken America up a bit — and they've got away with it because they're incredible. If Damon whatsisname came out and said all that "wanna be a star" stuff, it wouldn't work. I loved it when [Albarn] said he didn't really care about America. What bullshit. Anybody in this business cares about America.'

And there is the cult of the Gallagher brothers. On an American tour at the end of 1995, Oasis were asked to sign a poster for a band. Liam signed it, 'From the star of the stage', Noel signed it 'From the owner of the star of the stage'.

I gather that the UK looks upon Oasis as archetypal bad boys, but over here they're seen like wimp troubadours. At best, the Gallagher brothers' scrapes give them the aura of plucky Dickensian chimney sweeps.

US critic, gavin edwards

Noel might say the 'big dream is to be U2, not a little Britpop phenomenon, which is what we are now', but this doesn't mean the band haven't had moments of defeatism. In March 1995, during an American tour, Noel told the *Observer,* 'If someone said, you can go home now, I'd go. I don't think it's possible for a British band to be big in America anymore.'

When Oasis signed to Epic in America it was Griffiths, David Massey, head of A&R at Epic, Alan McGee of Creation and the band's manager, Marcus Russell, who decided on a plan with which to attack America. 'We put out the first album a bit after the UK,' recalls Griffiths. 'We knew that there was going to be a second album very quickly, in October, so our approach was very much to use the first album as a way of introducing the band. We knew we didn't have to go and drain every single drop of sales out of it.

'They came and toured,' he continues, discussing Oasis' earliest American gigs, 'and they started off playing lots of really smelly, horrible clubs, which they really needed to do. They hated it, but it really worked because it sold them to the media and to the kids.

'They kept coming back at regular intervals, and we did so well with "Live Forever", which sold about 500,000 records. We did a new video for that, in fact we had to redo most of the videos to make them more MTV-friendly, which the band was suspicious but cooperative about. Then we came back with "Morning Glory" as a single. Maybe we shouldn't have gone for that track but it did 250,000 copies and it showed a much rockier side of Oasis. We didn't want to come straight out with "Wonderwall" and go to pop radio because it was important that we maintained the fan base and the alternative side of it.

Liam in the USA.

Liam in rare motion.

Oasis must die. Do not buy Oasis records. They come to rape and pillage our women and invade America.

courtney love

Noel flying solo.

Back at the Brits. Liam with his date for the night, Patsy Kensit, February 1996.

'Then obviously "Wonderwall" became a multi-format smash. The next single's going to be "Champagne Supernova", so we're out of synch with the rest of the world again. It's very epic, Noel Gallagher is going to be the new Jim Steinman of rock music.'

Although Noel Gallagher would probably have preferred not to be compared to Jim Steinman by the head of his American record company (Steinman scripted most of Meatloaf's catalogue of songs), he must have been happy with the reception his band were being given.

I **can't** say if they'll be as big as the **Beatles**, but they could be one of the **biggest** bands of all time. They **can** be as **big** as they **wanna** be.

No meet-and-greets

'Oasis are playing rock'n'roll. It's not the dirty, distorted vocal grunge we're used to,' says Matt Costello, a DJ on a St Louis alternative radio station. 'We play "Wonderwall" once every three days. Even AOR stations play it. I can't say if they'll be as big as the Beatles, but they could be one of the biggest bands of all time. They can be as big as they wanna be.'

Noel is also happy to 'play the game', as he puts it. But only to a point. 'I don't give a fuck about meeting

some guy from Tower Records, the territory of Bog-arse, Ohio, who says he'll display our records better if we meet his wife and talk to him,' says Noel about the American-born tradition of meet-and-greet. '"I really want you to know what a great job I'm doing for your band,"' says Noel about the type of chat he is confronted with at such events. 'I just say, "You're paid to do a great job, you fucking idiot!" Bands come over here and because the band before did meet-and-greets, it's expected they'll do them too. Well, some one will say to the next lot of bands, "Oasis never did them, so you don't have to."'

Oasis have also used America as an opportunity to play some of their new tunes in sound checks. 'There's one called "My Big Mouth" — some of the people in the press will love that,' says Noel about one of the two new songs he is working on at the time of writing. 'There's another one, but I'm not sure what the title is because I haven't finished the lyrics,' he adds. 'We rehearsed on the day of the Brits, because we had fuck all better to do and all the band was in London. We weren't rehearsing for anything in particular, so we just got in there. I've got loads of songs written and I just wanted to see what they sounded like with the band, so we done 'em. They're probably going to be singles, actually.'

Witnessing Oasis in America, music writer Paolo Hewitt scribbles down some more of the lyrics for 'My Big Mouth': 'Where angels fly/You won't play... I'll put on my shoes/Walking slowly down the hall of fame'. The other song Paolo describes as being 'in the same vein, fast and melodic, proof that Noel has reverted back to writing on his electric guitar. That said, either song could easily have been penned years ago and only now brought out to play'.

Whether they were ready to play them or not, neither of these two songs were played when Oasis returned to the UK after the American tour to play the biggest two gigs of their career, at Manchester City Football club ground, Maine Road.

Alan White beating his skins.

It has just been phenomenal, there has never been anything to compare with it. We have already been talking to the Guinness Book of Records people.

The Maine chance

For the last weekend of April, 1996, Oasis came home. They returned to Britain's first music city, to play its second football stadium, Maine Road. The home to Manchester City FC can squeeze in 40,000 for a show. Oasis weren't the first band to play there. Rod Steward, Mike and The Mechanics, the Rolling Stones, Prince had all played this stadium. But none like Oasis did. Never has Maine Road witnessed such unabashed idolatry. The fans — from the early arrivers at the front to the lone groovers at the back — were truly 'mad for it'. Packed up tight, they

111

Noel with girlfriend Meg.

moved, cheered and sang as one, affording a band that had grown up down the road an all-conquering moment.

At first Oasis had only scheduled to play the Sunday night, but when tickets went on sale on February 8, 1996, they sold out in record time, and so an earlier show on Saturday was added. All the first 40,000 tickets shifted in seventy minutes, making it the fastest ever sell-out in British music history. Tickets were only available in the north of England — more of a gesture for their home-town fans than a discrimination against any others — and competition to get hold of them was intense.

'The ticket queue went right round the block. Oasis have been our best-selling act all year, but I have never seen anything like this,' said Manchester's HMV spokesperson about the lust for admission.

Snoasis. Noel in Oasis, March, 1996.

Another Manchester ticket outlet, Virgin Megastore, confounded fans who had queued through the night. At eight in the morning the gathered hundreds were informed that they should be at the back of the store. There was a mass stampede to the rear of the building and many fans lost their places. 'It was crazy,' says one jostled fan. 'There were some people who were asleep at the time, having queued all night, and then suddenly it was pandemonium.'

Phone lines to all the ticket agencies were so clogged that delegates attending a communications conference at Manchester educational institute UMIST were informed that fans rang a local ticket agency at a rate of 85,000 calls a minute, causing serious problems for other phone users on the same exchange. Even before the box-office opened for the second gig, touts were outside

The passenger. Noel might own a Rolls, but he can't drive it.

agencies selling tickets for the Sunday at £50, almost three times their face value. Oasis purposely kept the £17.50 price lower than one they could have commanded. 'We came from the dole queue,' says Noel about this altruistic gesture, 'so we know it's heartbreaking not to be able to afford to listen to your favourite band.' The combined sales of £1.4 million was good news for part-promoters, Manchester's SJM concerts.

'It has just been phenomenal,' said SJM's Rob Ballantyne on discovering the pace at which the tickets had gone. 'It beat Simply Red at Old Trafford, and there has never been anything to compare with it. We have already been talking to the Guinness Book Of Records people.'

And as he faced the sun he cast no shadow: 'Cast No Shadow'.

Sponsored by Oasis

For Oasis, playing the Manchester City Ground was one more realization of the many dreams they had when their career was just beginning. At the close of 1995 Noel Gallagher told *City Life* magazine that — as a massive City fan — he placed playing Maine Road on a parallel with writing and making the perfect LP. 'I went to see my first game in 1971 — I think it was City vs Newcastle — and I vowed that I would play centre-forward at Maine Road one day,' says Noel prior to the gig. 'Now I will settle for centre-stage.'

Previously the band's largest British event was the November Earls show. Such was the intensity of the

115

I **vowed** I would **play** centre-forward at **Maine Road** one day. **Now** I will **settle** for centre-stage.

noel

Noel with Oasis tribute band (of sorts) Northern Uproar.

Liam takes a fag break.

sound onstage and the audience's reception that Londoners in nearby Chelsea, Kensington and Fulham flooded police with reports that their homes were shaking. A spokesperson for the British Geological Survey said, 'No earthquakes or explosions were detected. We discovered that Oasis were playing in a concert at Earls Court Exhibition Centre, near the area where most the calls were received.'

'We've had this sort of thing happen before,' says David Redmayne of the global seismology unit in Edinburgh. 'There was speculation that very low-frequency noise was causing the shaking. Resonance plays a part in this; you just need to hit the right resonance of the building, something around seven Hertz, and the building starts shaking.'

Oasis didn't want to make the earth move around Maine Road. Aware that noise levels could be a problem the band got local residents on their side by giving them free tickets for the show.

Liam and Patsy escape to New York.

In February it was rumoured that Oasis might actually take over sponsorship of City from their long-term sponsors, Brother. City's £650,000 a year contract with Brother was expiring, and Oasis had already established other financial ties with the club. From Burnage, next door to Moss Side, the suburb in which Maine Road is situated, Oasis had already launched City's new £6 million training centre. And an executive dining area had been named The Oasis suite. There was some appeal for City to let Oasis replace Brother. With clever marketing, City/Oasis T-shirts could be sold all around the world. However, City chairman Francis Lee scotched speculation when he announced that Oasis 'have told me they will help us in any way possible on the merchandising side, but there is no way Oasis will be involved in our shirt sponsorship'. City were sticking with Brother.

Manchester City did approach Noel Gallagher to write a song for them, but Noel wasn't having any of that. 'I'm not going to sweat blood over a song unless it's for myself,' he says. 'Anyway, what can I get to rhyme with City?'

Facing the rivals

An Oasis song was reshaped for City, though. Not by the band but by City supporter and Oasis fan Simon Moorhead. 'I was on my way home listening to "Wonderwall" and I thought it would make the basis of a good football chant,' says Simon, 'I wrote some words, showed them to my mates and we all started singing it in the pub'. Convinced his song was a winner, and unimpressed by the more lewd ones that City had adopted, Simon began to distribute flyers containing the chant, and it has since been embraced at every City match. To the tune of "Wonderwall", it pays homage to City's mercurial midfielder Jeorgi Kinkladze, their goalkeeper Eike Immel and team manager Alan Ball. It goes: 'And all the runs that Kinky makes are winding/And

To **be** acknowledged as a **songwriter** has **definitely made** me more **content.** I know I will **leave** my **mark.**

noel, with the last word...for now

all the goals that city score are blinding/And there are many things that I would like to say to you/But I don't know how/ 'Cause Eike you gonna be the one that saves us/And after all, you're my Alan Ball'.

Rival Manchester United fans soon picked up on this song and offered their own less flattering interpretation which ended with the line: 'With Alan Ball, you'll win fuck all'.

The Gallaghers had always exhibited an open dislike for United. Before finding fame, Liam worked in the Formula One Car Valet service in Manchester where — it has been said — he threw water at Ryan Giggs, scratched Eric Cantona's Audi and rubbed wire wool on Paul Ince's BMW. 'I hate United. But I had nothing to do with it,' says Liam. 'I'm not a hooligan, but I can rant about my club, can't I? Football's a part of my life. It's up there with music and clothes.'

A week before Maine Road there were fears that the concerts wouldn't actually happen. Oasis had cancelled two shows on their American tour because Noel Gallagher had fallen ill with a virus. According to one report from the US, Noel had gone to visit an American doctor in Beverley Hills on the recommendation of songwriter/producer Burt Bacharach, with whom Noel was collaborating on a song. One supporting band who were scheduled but definitely would not be playing were Liverpool's Cast. Their guitarist, Liam Tyson, broke his shoulder while the band were touring Japan.

On the Saturday of the concert Noel was keen that any rivalry between City and United fans would not result in a riot — both United and City players were invited as special guests for the show. A statement said 'Oasis are inviting all the members of both the United and City squads, as Oasis feel this should be a celebration for the whole city.'

Invitations had also been sent to ex-Take That star Robbie Williams, Shaun Ryder and members of his band, Black Grape, members of M-People, Paul Weller, ex-Smith Johnny Marr, Bernard Sumner of New Order, all the Stone Roses, Liam's girlfriend Patsy Kensit, and stars from TV soaps Coronation Street and Brookside.

Cum on feel the noize

Manchester's city centre on the Saturday was gripped with Oasis fever to the extent that the *Manchester Evening News* ran the front-page headline: 'Oasis Mania Floods City'. All the record stores dedicated their display space to the band, and fans (plenty of whom were wearing the City top with 'Oasis' printed on the back) were milling about chanting their favourite Oasis songs. The atmosphere was good, and it mounted throughout the day until it finally burst the barriers of emotion the moment Oasis took the stage.

Supporting acts Ocean Colour Scene and the Manic Street Preachers were received with some enthusiasm, a

distraction for the crowd, some of whom had camped out since the early hours to guarantee a good view of the return of the celebrated Manchester band. The audience were teased by images of Oasis from massive screens flanking either side of the stage — the perfect stimulant for the vast crowd to start calling *their* band onstage. When, finally, they did arrive, the fans' reaction was an incredible sight to see. Oasis, without Liam for the first minutes, broke into their introduction, 'Swamp Song', and the stadium rocked. It was a momentum that picked up pace when Liam came out to take the vocals for 'Acquiesce'.

Movement onstage was kept to the obligatory minimum — no scissor kicks from Noel — and although the banter between the brothers was at best incomprehensible because of the incredible noise, every tune was a reminder of the perfect pop machine that Oasis had become. There were many memorable highlights. When Noel delivered the line 'good to be back' for 'Hello', you wondered if he had stolen it from Gary Glitter just for this particular event. Another B-side, 'Round Our Way', saw Liam's posture matched only in grandeur by the brass section. 'Champagne Supernova' was one thousand per cent Oasis, proof that the band had now transcended the point of being mere Beatles copyists. Noel's acoustic set ended with him singing 'Masterplan', then it all went electric again with 'Don't Look Back In Anger'. Liam returned to the stage for 'Live Forever', and they closed traditionally with 'I Am The Walrus'.

Oasis almost never do encores, but for Maine Road, on both days they returned to the stage with their cover of Slade's 'Cum On Feel The Noize', with Noel leaving the crowd on Saturday with the line: 'From the greatest band in the world, to the greatest audience in the world, goodnight.'

The two days days were not without onstage incidents. On Saturday Noel dedicated Supersonic to 'the kidnappers who say they're going to hold me ransom' in response to Manchester City mobsters who threatened violence and kidnap if they weren't given more tickets for the show. On the Sunday Noel and Liam argued about who was going to sing 'Whatever', resulting in Liam leaving the stage in a sulk.

On Sunday Ocean Colour Scene had their set disrupted when the crowd spotted Liam dancing on the highest terrace. Every time he made a move the crowd, who were now focusing on him, cheered. Only it wasn't Liam, it was his copy from the Oasis tribute band, No Way Sis.

The only element that spoiled the weekend came from robberies and localized violence outside on the streets of Moss Side around the stadium — Moss Side has a long history of street crime, and those many Oasis fans unaware of its unsavoury reputation made a fine target. On the Monday the *Manchester Evening News* ran with the front page headline 'Street Attack On Oasis fans'.

But for Oasis the band, Maine Road was the apotheosis of their career. There were no plans to tour further after this show for at least three months to allow Noel some time to write the band's third album, the traditionally difficult one. Not that Noel is worried.

'To be acknowledged as a songwriter has definitely made me more content. I know I will leave my mark,' he says about his current status. 'Even if I never write another song, I've written enough now. I've been a punter, a roadie, a pop star. Next? Junkie and ex-pop star I'd say.'

Liam does his angel impersonation.

December, 1988

Noel Gallagher recruited by Inspiral Carpets as roadie.

August 18th, 1991

Oasis play their first gig, at Manchester's Boardwalk. Noel, who has yet to join, is in the audience.

January 1992

Oasis play first gig with Noel, again at the Boardwalk. The first song they play is an instrumental version of Columbia.

July 1992

Oasis play their first live radio session for Mark Radcliffe, on his seminal Radio 5 show, Hit the North.

December 1992

Oasis record their first demo proper, Live Demonstration, in Liverpool.

18th May 1993

The band play at King Tut's Wah Wah Hut in Glasgow and Creation boss Alan McGee offers them a deal.

June 1993

Oasis' future manager, Marcus Russell, arrives at Manchester venue The Hop and Grape with Johnny Marr to see the band play.

October 22nd, 1993

Oasis sign to Creation for the UK and Sony for the rest of the world.

December 1993

Recording sessions in Liverpool produce 'Supersonic'.

January 1994 -

Radio 1 take the unprecedented step of play-listing 'Columbia', a single sided promo not commercial available.

18th February 1994

The band, minus Noel, are incarcerated in Holland for kicking off on a ferry.

March 1994

Oasis make their debut TV appearance, playing the cult Channel 4 series, *The Word*.

April 11th 1994

'Supersonic' is released. It reaches No. 31 in the British singles chart.

June 20th 1994

'Shakermaker' takes Oasis just outside the Top 10, to No. 11.

June 26th 1994

The band play the Glastonbury festival's *NME* stage. Here Liam asks the crowd, 'Are you gonna wake up, then, for some real songs?'

August 8th 1994

Oasis release 'Live Forever' and go to No. 10. Their plan to release one single every two months and achieve higher chart positioning each time is working.

August 29th 1994

Definitely Maybe, the debut album from Oasis takes the No. 1 slot in the British album charts. It is the fastest-selling debut of all time.

September 1994

Oasis do their first Japanese tour and are greeted with mania.

September 23rd 1994

Oasis play the first date of their slightly shaky first American tour.

October 10th 1994 -

Cigarettes And Alcohol reaches No. 7 in the UK charts.

December 19th 1994

Whatever gives Oasis their highest chart positioning to date, it goes to number 3.

January 1995

On his acoustic guitar Noel writes the bulk of the Oasis's second album.

January 23rd 1995

Oasis win Best Band, Best New Band, and Best Single for 'Live Forever' at NME Brat awards.

February 28th 1995

Oasis get Best New Band at Brit awards. Blur win four awards and dedicate their Best Band award to Oasis.

March 1995

'Live Forever' is at the top of the American college charts, and *Definitely Maybe* has sold over 220,000 copies.

April 24th 1995

Oasis have their first No. 1 hit with Some Might Say.

April 27th 1995

Drummer Tony McCarroll makes his last appearance with Oasis on Top Of The Pops. He is replaced that week by Alan White.

May 8th 1995 -

Oasis enter the Rockfield Studios to record their second album.

June 23rd 1995

Robbie Williams from Take That joins Oasis onstage at the Glastonbury festival.

August 14th 1995

Oasis release 'Roll With It' and Blur release 'Country House', sparking the big pop tiff of the nineties. Oasis have to settle for No. 2 slot.

September 1995

Bass player Guigsy leaves the band citing nervous exhaustion.

October 2nd 1995

(What's They Story) Morning Glory? is released. It goes straight in at No. 1.

October 17th 1995

Temporary bassist Scott McLeod leaves the band in the middle of an American tour.

October 30th 1995

'Wonderwall' is released, taking the No. 2 slot a week later.

November 4th & 5th 1995

Oasis play the biggest indoor European gig on record at the Earls Court Exhibition Centre. Crowd capacity on each night is 20,000.

December 1995

'Wonderwall' enters the *Billboard* charts in America at No. 21, *Definitely Maybe* has now sold in excess of 500,000 copies.

February 1996

Tickets for the Oasis gig at Manchester City ground Maine Road are released. 80,000 are shifted in record time.

February 19th 1996

'Don't Look Back In Anger' is released, the first single release with Noel not Liam on vocals. It goes to No. 1.

April 27th, 28th

Oasis play their two dates at Maine Road, and the crowd are 'mad for it'.

Singles.

Supersonic (31)
April 11th, 1994 (CRE 176)
b. Take Me Away, I Will Believe, Columbia.

Shakermaker (11)
June 20th, 1994 (CRE 182)
b. D'Yer Wanna Be A Spaceman?,Alive, Bring it on Down.

Live Forever (10)
August 8th, 1994 (CRE 185)
b. Up In The Sky, Cloudburst, Supersonic.

Cigarettes and Alcohol (7)
October 10th, 1994 (CRE 190)
b. I Am The Walrus, Listen Up, Fade Away.

Whatever (3)
December 19th, 1994 (CRE 195)
b. (It's Good) To Be Free, Half The World Away, Slide Away.

Some Might Say (1)
April 24th, 1995 (CRE 204)
b. Talk Tonight, Acquiesce, Headshrinker

Roll With It (2)
August 14th, 1995 (CRE 212)
b. It's Better People, Rockin' Chair, Live Forever

Wonderwall (2)
October 30th, 1995 (CRE 215)
b. Round Are Way, The Swamp Song, The Masterplan.

Don't Look Back in Anger (1)
February 19th, 1996 (CRE 221)
b. Step Out, Underneath The Sky, Cum On Feel The Noize.

Albums

Definitely Maybe (1)
August 29th, 1994 (CRECD/LP 169)

Rock N Roll Star.
Shakermaker.
Live Forever.
Up in the Sky.
Columbia.
Supersonic.
Bring It on Down.
Cigarettes and Alcohol
Digsy's Dinner.
Slide Away.
Married With Children.

(What's The Story) Morning Glory (1)
Oct 2nd, 95 (CRECD/LP 189)

Hello.
Roll With It.
Wonderwall.
Don't Look Back in Anger.
Hey Now.
Some Might Say.
Cast No Shadow.
She's Electric.
Morning Glory.
Champagne Supernova.

index